the **actor** *and the* **camera**

the **actor**
and the **camera**

MALCOLM TAYLOR

A & C Black • London

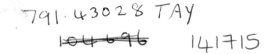
For my daughters Ellen and Katie
and my good friend John Fielding

First published in 1994 by
A & C Black (Publishers) Limited
35 Bedford Row, London WC1R 4JH

ISBN 0–7136–3901–6

© 1994 Malcolm Taylor

Published simultaneously in the U.S.A. by Heinemann
A Division of Reed Publishing (USA) Inc.
361 Hanover Street
Portsmouth, NH. 03801–3912
Offices and Agents throughout the world

Distributed in Canada by Reed Books Canada,
75 Clegg Road, Markham, Ontario L6G 1A1

ISBN 0-435-08639-1

CIP catalogue records for this book are available from
the British Library and the Library of Congress.

Typeset in 10½ on 12½ pt Linotron Sabon by
Florencetype Limited, Kewstoke, Avon
Printed and bound in Great Britain by Biddles Ltd,
Guildford Surrey

Contents

Acknowledgements

I'd like to thank Frank Dickens for his cartoons; Vere Lorrimer for getting me into this mess in the first place; Richard Martin, Christopher Denys, Darren Little, Bernard Holley and Mike Dormer for their help and advice; Lindsay Anderson, Roger Carey, Ralph Jago, David Jason, Leonard Lewis, and Gill Titchmarsh for giving their time for interviews; my wife Annie, for invaluable suggestions and corrections; BFI Stills Posters and Designs for library and re-printing services; Christopher Staines for permission to use his C.V.

The publishers join with me in thanking the following for kindly giving their permission to publish their photographs:

Yorkshire Television/BBC for *Campion and EastEnders*
Yorkshire Television/Thames for *The Bill*
(The above featured in YTV's *A Day in the Life of Television*)
BBC Television for *One Foot In The Grave* and *Alexandra Palace*
Granada Television for *Coronation Street*
Topaz Productions for corporate stills
Paramount Pictures for *If*
Frank Connor for *Britannia Hospital*
Yorkshire Television for *A Touch of Frost*
Anglia Television for *A Quiet Conspiracy*

Fast Foreword

I was originally commissioned to write a book about camera acting technique, but somehow, when I sat down and started to scribble, I found myself wanting to let you in on all the little bits and pieces of information that seem to shroud 'the Business' in unnecessary mystique. Sometimes I think it suits the purposes of 'them upstairs' to keep actors in the dark about things which don't directly have to do with performance, and having groped about in the dark myself in my early acting days, I hope I am now in a position to shed a little light on matters that I believe you really ought to know. So although you'll find a lot of helpful acting hints within these covers, I'd like to think the book will also go some way towards satisfying your curiosity about such things as how to set about finding a suitable drama school, how to join Equity, how *Coronation Street* works, what inter-active video means, what the difference is between a producer and a director, etc., etc.

Much of the book is given over to the views and opinions of others, whose knowledge and experience in their various fields is far greater than mine; to a large extent I feel I've 'directed' the book rather than 'written' it. I make no apologies for this because I don't pretend to be a writer – or teacher for that matter.

I've simply attempted to filter, edit and communicate some information and ideas that may be of assistance if you are a student or young professional, or simply satisfy your curiosity if you're a 'tele buff' or enthusiastic amateur. Personally I would buy the book just for the sheer wit of Frank Dicken's drawings!

Chapter One
Thinking Things Through

Stillness is probably the most important quality an actor needs to possess if he or she is to be successful in the craft of acting for the camera; stillness not only of the mind and eye but also of the body. For unlike the theatre, where physical, bravura performances can, in the right role, be effective, the 'frame' of the camera doesn't permit the actor the same freedom. The most captivating quality the camera has to offer an audience is its ability to capture subtleties of expressions and thoughts. A few people, often beginners, sense this and use their natural instinct, but most trained actors, who may only have experienced the projection technique demanded of theatre, will have to think again.

IT'S DIFFICULT TO
KEEP STILL WHEN
IT'S A WALK-ON
PART...

The camera has the ability to enquire and probe to such an extent that an actor either lacking in true depth of emotion, or ill at ease (i.e. unaware of *what* he should be thinking at any given time) with the character he is playing, will be found out. So it is necessary for an actor to have assimilated the character he is playing to such an extent that to all intents and purposes he *is* that character.

This is not to say that people who are normally considered to be 'playing themselves' are not true actors. On the contrary, such actors – and most of the stars of the big screen fall into this category – have merely tuned their brains to reproduce an aspect of themselves, real or imagined, which fits the requirement of the current role. Indeed it is often more difficult for the imaginative, truly inventive, 'character' actor to achieve star status in films and television, for audiences find comfort and reassurance in recognising their favourite performers. They do not usually take kindly, for instance, to their favourite comedy star suddenly turning up as a mass murderer. 'Versatile' actors are usually therefore to be found in good supporting parts, and often, because there are more roles readily available to them, they will find more true acting satisfaction, and make the better living over the course of their career.

In television, many actors find 'stardom' almost by chance. This is almost invariably due to exposure in a long running situation comedy series, soap opera, or series, which proves popular with viewers. Many of these actors live to curse the day they first found favour in this manner, for as the series wanes, and then dies, so do their careers. Some, on the other hand, either by careful management, luck, or sheer talent, find such a series a useful trampoline which bounces them on to bigger, often better, opportunities.

Few actors are given a real choice between remaining a relatively unknown, but working actor, and being catapulted into television stardom because of exposure in some series. But if there is ever a likelihood of it happening to you, it's worth pausing for thought before signing the contract for yet another series of the same. You might find yourself condemned to wearing the straight-jacket of the character for life. On the other hand you might think, like Jean Alexander, who played Hilda Ogden in *Coronation Street*, (and had been a provincial reper-

CORPSE DAGGER — DAGGER — CORPSE

They do not take kindly, for instance, to their favourite comedy star suddenly turning up as a mass murderer

tory actress for years before she got the offer) 'Thank God, this is a bit of security I wasn't expecting – now I can really settle down and enjoy myself.' The important thing is to be aware of what's going on around you, and try to take as much responsibility for your career as you can. You'll probably find there won't be that many opportunities!

To sharpen your observation, try, when you next watch an old television play or film, to spot the different categories of actors who are taking part. It's well worth noting the actors who have remained durable, gone on to become stars, or simply disappeared.

Watching other actors at work is one of the best ways of learning your craft. And watching them on the box or on the screen is even better, for you can see their performances over and over again – the same performances. Unlike the theatre, where performances can, and often do, change every night, a film or television performance can be retrieved and screened long after an actor's death, so once it's in the can that's his lot! A frightening thought isn't it? Watch the way the actors move,

You can see their performances over and over again . . .

note the amount of projection they use, look into their eyes and always ask the question 'Do I believe in them?' If not, your next question should be 'Why not?' Perhaps you thought they were too fat or thin for the part, or that they should have had more hair or be of a younger or older age. Yes, perhaps. But because we know ourselves to be fallible in a physical sense we are usually very forgiving of such shortcomings – indeed we often feel reassured when a plain man gets the pretty girl, or vice versa. No, more often than not your suspension of belief will be because they have been asked to deliver cretinous lines in a totally unconvincing script, or have not got under the skin of their characters – and their eyes are empty. If it's the former then they were either broke at the time they were offered the part (in which case they takes the money and suffer the consequences), their judgement of the script was impaired, or they were rendered impotent by a rotten director. But if it's the latter they can be judged to have failed you; they may well judge that they have failed themselves too. Be that as it may, it's the audience that an actor is serving, not himself. After all people are giving their money, or at least their time, for you to transport them out of themselves into *your* world, so you must do your best to get it right.

Of course the truth, or reality, you invest in a character is always subject to the style of production you are in. For instance, the heightened, manic reality of *Roseanne* is very different from the gritty reality of *The Godfather*, and one's perception of truth is coloured by the style of presentation. We will discuss these differing styles in later chapters, but whether an actor sustains belief and conviction *within the given style* remains the only criteria by which his performance can be judged.

Acting is a natural talent. It's often said that all children can act but most lose this ability as they get older, possibly through inhibition or lack of self-confidence as they approach puberty. Nevertheless, most people retain an ability, to some degree, to imitate or impersonate their fellows, and the difference between a talent for impersonation and a talent for acting is worth examining. Not all actors are good impersonators, but some so called actors are nothing but. And, just to confuse things even further, some extremely good actors, when called upon to play well-known public figures, confuse the two and give a brilliant impersonation instead of a carefully thought out and assimi-lated performance. Often they are upset when the reviews they receive are less than fulsome. While impersonations can some-times pass for performances in the theatre, because of the dis-tance involved, they can never convince when the actors *eyes* are on display, for they are the give-away to what is going on in the brain. So while it is perfectly acceptable for an actor to tag on a few well-known hand gestures to his interpretation of a personality, neither the gesture nor the voice, without moti-vation, will carry conviction.

Say, for instance, you are called upon to play a member of the Royal Family, it would be very important for you to invent and motivate a personality for these little known but often seen characters. An audience will accept your characterisation and forgive the fact that you do not look quite right and are not the best impersonator; what they won't accept is an empty imper-sonation – even as a variety act.

Unless an actor has a firm and clear idea of his character before he presents himself on the set he is lost. Never rely on help being at hand on the day. Everyone, from the director to the lowliest assistant, is likely to be so concerned with doing their own job properly that actors are often their last consideration. I once heard an extremely well-known director, who shall be nameless, say to an actress requesting direction in the playing of a scene, 'It's no good asking me honey, I'm just taking the snaps; you're the actress'. Remember, be prepared.

Having said that acting is a natural talent, the effectiveness of that talent can be improved by working on one's technique. Apart from improving one's voice, movement and physical prowess, there are a number of 'tricks' you will pick up as you experiment and observe, such as the most effective way to eat your way through a scene (making sure you get the sort of food you can cope with, planning your pauses, etc.) but be careful you don't start substituting technique for thought, because the camera will catch you 'at it'!

I had the honour, as a young actor, of working on stage with Sir Laurence Olivier, whose technique was superb. At one point, during a performance of *Coriolanus*, as he turned upstage in anguish, a bangle he was wearing slipped down his arm. Calm as a cucumber, he dropped his characterisation, 'Oh, fuck', he said for our amusement, calmly replacing it. Turning back to the oblivious audience he 'switched on' again. His theatre technique was superb but some of his critics believe his screen performances, though fascinating, never had the necessary depth for the cinema. Meryl Streep has also been criticised for approaching her roles from a technical point of view. It's a subjective opinion and doubtless you will have yours, but not many stars have given as much pleasure in such a variety of roles as Olivier and Streep.

The most effective way of improving your ability is through genuine self-knowledge; keep 'up-dating' yourself as you develop and mature. It's very important for an actor to see himself as others see him. Don't waste your time agonising over parts you clearly aren't right for. By and large, if some element of the character isn't within you, or that you could easily imagine *could* be within you, you aren't right for it. So concentrate on realistic goals if you want to achieve a modicum of success, and more importantly, contentedness. Although it often seems, in the acting profession, that life is all about 'getting on' and 'playing the right part', it's a very small part of life as a whole, so don't make yourself unhappy by being unrealistically ambitious. Don't forget (and this is specially applicable if you become famous) who you are, and start living a fantasy life *for real!* And above all retain your sense of humour – God knows you'll need it often enough!

Acting in the theatre, particularly in repertory, will give you more opportunity to identify your strengths and weaknesses than being plunged straight into film or television. So if you get the chance, opt for as much varied theatrical experience as you can before succumbing to the blandishments (money!) of the media. Albert Finney, for instance, turned down many lucrative offers and elected to go to Birmingham rep for two years, 'to practice', after he left RADA (Royal Academy of Dramatic Art). Like managers with a new play, it's sensible, if you have the opportunity, to give yourself the space to experiment and 'try yourself out' in the provinces, before exposing yourself to a wider public.

Different aspects of the media will make different demands of you. But before discussing these, and hopefully giving you a few tips on how to cope with them, let's deal with a few basics.

If the obvious difference between acting for the camera and acting for the theatre is one of size and detail, it follows that it is about economy; economy of movement and expression – which brings us back to my initial point – a practised stillness. But it's as well to be aware that your performance is then manipulated by others. In the theatre, at the end of the day, director notwithstanding, an actor comes face to face with his audience, and is therefore in charge, or at least responsible for, his performance. Not so in television. The director, post performance, will then select which parts of it he wants to be seen by the audience, so to a large extent your performance is controlled by him. Feature film is another matter, for it is usually the producer (I'll explain the difference later), who assumes final control. (In fact, as more and more television drama is subject to the power of the 'Almighty Buck', artistic considerations are often given a back seat, and decisions traditionally made by the director are increasingly devolving to the producer, who can, if he chooses, save money on a director's fee, by editing the show himself.)

'Ah yes', I hear you say, 'But how can a director change the performance I give? After all, if I play the part, even if he cuts a bit, he'll still have to show them what I did, so it can't make that much difference. I might lose a line or two, but that's all.' Wrong! Let's take a scene shot on a single camera as a first example. It is invariably photographed from different angles, and unlike the theatre, where an audience sees the entire action containing all the actors, in television and film the director has the ability to edit out great chunks of the original scene, cut out speeches he doesn't think work in retrospect, and generally change the entire emphasis. Further, he also decides who (or what) – it could be a shot of anything you'd like to name – will be featured during the course of a given speech or piece of action. He might also decide that he doesn't like your voice and get another artist to 'dub' yours (though this tends to be practised more in film). So although you may have played your big emotional speech to camera, there's absolutely no guarantee that that's what you will see at the end of the day. Even scenes shot with several cameras (see Chapter 7, page 79) still present a great amount of choice. In fact it's extremely likely that your speech *will* be broken up in some way. The director may well decide, quite rightly, that the effect of what you're saying has on somebody else is far more important than your own dear features. So don't be upset or thrown by this when you come to view the finished programme, and try to be as objective as possible. Similarly, remember, when you are doing 'reverses' (listening to someone else), that it may well be *your* reaction that ends up on the screen, so always play your scene to the best of your ability when 'off' camera so that your partner has the benefit of your performance to react to. (Richard Harris once told me he had to pretend a mop head was Marlon Brando when doing 'reverses' on *Mutiny on the Bounty*.) Some, fortunately few, stars refuse to act off camera for someone else's reactions – presumably in the hope that their partner's reactions will therefore be so unconvincing that they will be discarded in the edit. Make no mistake, it can be a bitchy business!

As a rule of thumb, when performing in a 'realistic' piece, be natural. Let the characteristics of your assumed personality emerge as simply as you would your own. If you need to increase your vocal level ('more voice') you can be sure that the sound recordist will tell the director, who, in turn will tell you.

CUT TO SHOT OF LEFT SHOE

The director will then select which parts of the performance he wants to be seen by the audience

When you're more experienced you will often find that you are able to judge this perfectly for yourself. Many actors also strike up a rapport with the cameraman and sound recordist too, who can often save a lot of time by giving them 'the nod' if they are moving about too much or under vocalising. Secure directors usually welcome such short cuts.

This brings us to your relationship with a director. Ideally you will love and trust him or her (an increasing number of successful film and television directors are women), but in practice, you will find you get on better with some than others. When I was acting myself, I found only a handful who could communicate with me in the way I had experienced in the theatre. Directors come from many backgrounds: technical, journalistic, research, documentary, and only a few from the theatre, so you don't necessarily talk the same language. Directors are therefore often very tentative, not to say frightened, of actors, and don't know instinctively when and how to be of help. Even more reason to do your homework before you work with them. There's no doubt that a good 'Actor's Director' is worth his weight in gold to you, but they are few and far between. You should assume (you can always be pleasantly surprised) that your director will be more interested in getting the technicalities right and doing the show within the alloted time span than he will be in your 'search for the truth'. But even the most sympathetic and helpful director can be driven insane by actors who are constantly seeking praise and attention – the 'look at me' variety I call them – so don't expect fulsome praise at the end of every scene; if you don't get a note assume you're on the right track. Yes, make sure you feel secure and comfortable, for without your contribution a drama is meaningless, but do appreciate all the additional demands being made of the director and try to keep out of his hair if you can see he's distracted by problems in other areas. Finally, I know that actors need some feed-back, and all I can say is that if you aren't getting it from the director then you've got to get it from somebody else – anybody – who happens to be around, and whose judgement you can trust. It is, after all, your name on the end credits.

Talking of end credits, did you know that television companies, in their increasingly desperate struggle to keep viewers tuned to their station, are trying to dream up ways of doing away with end (your!) credits? That's why they whizz by so quickly on American programmes that you haven't time to read them. Prepare to register your protest if you're ever asked to do so. There must be enough time for your name to be noticed by potential employees.

Now, as to the differences between the titles 'Director' and 'Producer'. In television, the producer is employed by the company making the programme (either a broadcasting company, like the BBC or CBS, or an independent production company, like MGM or Cinema Verity). The producer is in overall charge and is often responsible for hiring the director. He will usually be the person with whom the writer will work initially, introducing the director to the creative team as and when he is appointed. The producer is usually in charge of the budget – though sometimes this can be in the hands of an executive producer (who is, hopefully, an arms length away from the production process). You will find a lot of 'usually's' and 'often's' in these descriptions because nothing is absolutely cut and dried, and every set up has its own working arrangements.

The director is nominally in charge of the artistic content of the show. It's his job to hire the actors, usually in consultation with the producer, conduct rehearsals, if any, provide the camera script (see Chapter 7) and supervise the editing.

In theory the producer fulfils the same role in feature films as in television, but in practice he exercises much more control in feature films. As I mentioned earlier, unless the director has a prior agreement with the company (rare), the producer will have the 'final cut' (make the final editing decisions). Indeed he may well take all meaningful decisions throughout the shooting process, and the director can almost be reduced to a cipher. This is particularly true of American film production. Broadly speaking, he who controls the purse gets to pull the strings – so the bigger the purse the more strings pulled.

Here is a *very* simplified guide of the production process, which may help you visualise how your contribution fits in. You can see that you're at the centre, surrounded on all sides!

EXECUTIVE PRODUCER = PRODUCER = CO-PRODUCERS
|
WRITER
|
DIRECTOR
|
CASTING
|
CAMERA, SOUND ETC.   = **ACTORS** = MAKE-UP, COSTUMES ETC.
|
COMPLETE PROGRAMME FOOTAGE
|
EDITOR
|
SOUND DUB (EFFECTS, RE-VOICE)
|
COMPLETED PROGRAMME
|
AUDIENCE

When you are on a shoot try to be aware of the relationships that are going on around and steer a clear course through the middle. You certainly don't want to get caught up in any off-screen bickering or back-stabbing, because that will involve taking sides, and you certainly can't afford to do that. Although obvious, it's worth mentioning that the little guy running around taking the dinner orders today might be your most important employer tomorrow!

If acting for television needs to be minimal, then acting for the movies needs to be imperceptible. It's all about faces and eyes; thought, not script-based. Most of the big names in movies seem to have almost impassive expressions. If Clint Eastwood raises an eyebrow it probably means he's going to shoot someone; if Meryl Streep smiles it probably means she's in love. An exaggeration, of course, but you get my drift. Because the cinema screen is so large, expressions need to be that much smaller. Thought behind the eyes is what counts. Thought projection is what screen acting is all about.

People often ask me what I consider to be the difference between television and film. The prime, and obvious difference is that film is a physical medium – the *solid light* image is stored and edited on a negative that produces prints, while the television *electronically scanned line* images are produced, stored and edited on receptive video tape, (the greater the number of lines scanned, the sharper the image – hence the improved quality of High Definition Television – over 1,000 lines compared to the usual 625). Prime *film* camera lenses (those specifically designed to encompass a fixed angle of sight, as opposed to zoom lenses, which distort to a certain extent) operate much like the human eye. The point at which the cameraman focuses them remains incredibly sharp while closer and more distant images gradate in direct ratio to the focal point. Television camera lenses, on the other hand (especially the popular, versatile zooms) tend to have less gradation of focus and therefore produce 'flatter' pictures, though they have improved beyond recognition in recent years. That's why films have a greater sense of reality – the human brain recognises more easily the image closest to the one produced by its own eye.

But there is another important difference – the effect these images have on the audience when viewed in the environment for which they were designed. The reason I often fall asleep while watching television is partly due to the fact that I usually

End credits whizz by so quickly on American television programmes you don't have time to read them

watch television in my own environment, with some lights on. I'm relaxed, so if I'm tired and slumped in my favourite chair, I can easily nod off, particularly if the programme doesn't hold my interest. Television programmes, however good they might be, still have to compete with many other domestic distractions. Even a first rate film is considerably diminished when shown on television. The screen is small and is intruding into *my* world, not I into *its*. This is the key difference I think. In the cinema I never go to sleep. Walk out maybe. This is because I tend to be alert in an alien environment. I'm sitting in the dark and the light and size of the screen attracts and dominates my attention to the exclusion of all else. Because film technology has advanced to such a state of realism (even if it's portraying fantasy it has the ability to convince me that it's real) I'm sucked into its world.

It's therefore a lot easier for an actor to make a lasting impact in the cinema. Most 'television actors' will agree to play quite small parts in a film because they know this. Film appearances can, and often do, enhance their reputation, but not their talent. If it's dubious, film exposure will only confirm the suspicions.

Right, so you want to be a movie star. Let's make a start . . .

Chapter Two
Teaching and Training

In common with many directors, over the years I've been asked to take classes and even devise training courses on an ad hoc basis, but other than that, I've never really given training much thought, until I was asked to write this book.

I'd assumed, wrongly as it turns out, that there would be extensive television training given to students, at least in our major drama schools. When I was at RADA in the late fifties, television was more or less in its infancy, but even then we were a little critical that the only media training we were given was radio technique, which consisted of one session a week in the final year. There was not a word about the oncoming flood of television drama that was bursting upon us.

You can imagine my surprise, therefore, when I came to research the training on offer, thirty five years on, that I found so little *real* interest. I also found that a couple of our 'top' schools were quite reluctant to enter into a discussion about their ability to train actors for film and television (guilt?). I got the distinct impression that they wished I'd go away. I did.

Although it is true to say that all the drama schools that run courses accredited by the National Council for Drama Training devote some of their curriculum to acting for the camera, none that I questioned, in my opinion, devote enough. As far as I am aware only ALRA (Academy of Live and Recorded Arts) and the Bristol Old Vic Theatre School have dedicated studios and equipment available in house, though Richard Martin, in charge of Television Training at Mountview Theatre School, is hoping to introduce studio facilities as soon as possible. There isn't a single drama school that puts the emphasis first and foremost on screen training, which is incredible when one thinks that any 'living' that is to be had from the acting profession these days largely stems from film and television work of one kind or another.

Although I appreciate that the acting process is basically common to all media, techniques and indeed actors' abilities are not. And in spite of the fact that equipment and studios are more costly than rooms and stages, I personally think our main drama schools need a good kick to get them into the fast approaching twenty first century. Screens of all shapes and sizes have been with us for the last fifty years, and it's high time we had a Royal Academy of Screen Arts, if, for the most part, our schools can't do better than hire in a camcorder once or twice a week, and lay on a workshop or two under the guise of television training. Could do better!

Small wonder then, that across the pond, our American colleagues, who have a plethora of dedicated screen schools, are consistently turning out well-trained young screen actors, who by-pass theatre altogether. (*The American Film Institute Guide to College Courses in Film and Television* by Peterson's Guide Book order Department, P.O. Box 978, Edison, NJ 08817, will provide you with a comprehensive list of screen schools.) We, on the other hand, seem almost to dismiss screen acting ability as second rate. The truth is, that some actors are more suited to the screen than the stage, but without proper training facilities they will be judged by the wrong set of criteria and may be overlooked as 'having no voice', 'lacking in projection', or 'too small in characterisation'.

I well remember Pierce Brosnan joining our company at the Theatre Royal York, when I was artistic director in the mid-seventies. He was employed as 'ASM' and 'small parts'. Although he acquitted himself well and was a very pleasant young man, his performances were best viewed from the front of the stalls, (except for his skeletal dance in *The Wizard of Oz*, which carried to the back of the gallery!). His leave of the company coincided with our annual party, and I remember him coming up to me and asking how I thought he'd performed. I told him that I thought his work was splendid, but 'a bit too small for this theatre', (it seats over a thousand) adding, 'if you're very lucky, with your looks and charm of the devil, you could be a film star'. His move to America shortly afterwards gave him the break that brought him justifiable success.

Because of our historical theatre background, I think the English tend to 'think theatre', whereas the Americans 'think movies'. To a greater or lesser extent, this surely reflects on the comparative status of the two industries.

I talked to Ralph Jago, the Principal of the Webber Douglas Academy of Dramatic Art, and Chairman of the Conference of Drama Schools, and sought his opinion of the screen training his establishment currently offers. He was refreshingly frank.

M.T. Your school seems to do as much training for the screen as any I've come across, but even so it's not really a lot is it?

Jago No there isn't a lot. But I'll try to put you in the picture as far as we're concerned. We have an experienced director who does two workshops on single camera work, and we have just started an experiment this term with another director, who does a 'talking heads' project in which we take an audition piece, then take a minute out of it, and shoot it in a professional studio with professional camera and sound men. The single camera work covers techniques of acting unique to the medium; situations students will meet at commercial casting sessions, both with mime and improvisation with a partner. Scripts of a well-known 'soap opera' are given out, and rehearsed and recorded with students doing acting and technical roles. All these exercises are recorded and analysed.

With the 'Talking Heads' project the aim is to provide a VHS tape of an extract which expressly demonstrates the screen potential of the student; one minute to camera, filmed as one developing shot, with minimum 'props' if required. Action can either be directly to camera or to an unseen person. An experienced film crew instructs and oversees the proceedings. This a pilot project that I've not even seen yet. We hire everything here. We used to have a television studio but we had to give it up because of the problem of maintenance; we couldn't afford to have a full-time engineer. We try to concentrate on the workshops by focusing on the specific things they need to know. And we did a survey of ex-students who'd since had professional experience. . . Everybody concerned said they wanted more television workshops, they were thought to be good, but there wasn't enough of them . . . A lot of what was taught needed more emphasis and more practice. (At this point he consulted his notes.) These are the things that concerned

them most; a) the importance of tight framing; b) the importance of keeping energy levels up for continuity, and the
repetition of 'take' after 'take', and doing a scene out of
context after a lot of hanging around; c) keeping one's concentration going when the lighting engineers get in your way.

M.T. I don't think that's the way the lighting engineers see it!

Jago (chuckles) No, quite. . . then there's d) the studio atmosphere which can be awful, ie. very pressurised. Time is money,
and some felt they were not prepared for that pressure. . .
Then there's the mundane practicalities of having to walk over
things – especially camera tracks, and avoiding television
monitors. . . Managing to look natural, when told to turn
round and react immediately, especially in no more than two
'takes'; e) learning 'internal' rather than 'external' thinking;
f) learning to cope with a live studio audience – difficult to
know whether to play to camera or audience; g) sight reading,
as taught here, was considered good but they said they needed
a lesson with a really bad script!

M.T. Ah, you mean a *normal* one.

Jago You said it. They also felt that we should have at least
one workshop with a different director (we are doing) just to
suggest a different approach; have in a couple of directors to
talk or lecture, and that we should invite a well-known
television actor to come in and talk and be questioned. The
consensus was that we should have more television workshops and that most drama schools don't give enough television tuition, but what was taught was good.

M.T. So they think that even in a well-respected, and presumably fairly representative establishment, that there isn't
enough television training about?

Jago Yes. The problem is of course, cost; once you introduce
cameras and technicians and studios the whole thing becomes
much more expensive than actor training. So what you have
to do is not do your actor training on camera because it's
incredibly expensive, except for the bits you HAVE to, if you
see what I mean . . .

M.T. But it's camera training that's surely needed.

Jago But they must sort all their acting out first, and you can do that cheaply in the theatre. Once you've got your acting problems sorted out, then you can learn the other information. Secondly, the problem of cameras and equipment is maintenance. If you do have a studio, you would have to run it (unless you are a highly subsidised organisation like the National Film School – and that's for technicians not actors) by hiring that space out . . . Also a lot of the schools are traditionally located in small, scattered, premises, and can't deal with a central studio – there's no way we could deal with a TV studio in Kensington and Chelsea! In fact on this workshop, we went out to Greenwich University, and we used their fully professional studio. For the radio class, we went out to Bromley. So we go to a place which has the set-up and buy into it, basically. Personally, I find this works better than when we used our own equipment, which kept going wrong! Originally, we tried to make many 20–30 minute films, all hand held, on location (which cost us a lot of money), but we found that; a) nobody wanted to come and see them, and b) it was virtually impossible to ensure that every student was in a film. So we discovered that it was better to go to specific workshops covering specific things, such as acting in commercials, working with two cameras, short scenes, three-handed scenes, etc.

M.T. Is there room, do you think, for shared facilities for all the drama schools?

Jago No, that wouldn't work. I've had experience of drama schools trying to co-operate, and you spend endless amounts of time trying to re-schedule and in the end you give it up.

M.T. What about a drama school that is angled towards screen training?

Jago Yes, I think that would be a good idea . . . Yes, I could definitely see a school bent towards the screen, and *because* of that getting money to do it.

M.T. In some ways I feel that, just as the drama schools in the theatre have helped to keep the theatrical tradition strong

John Gorrie gives direction to actors Joss Ackland and Sarah Winman during the shoot of *A Quiet Conspiracy*. Note the tracks actors often have to negotiate

here, and have generated work, a school orientated towards film and television might feed the industry and prod it into doing more.

Jago I think this is very probably true . . . If you look through *Spotlight*, very few directors will be inspired by the photographs. These are the young people coming into the business, and hardly any them are camera aware. Most of the drama schools have bits of courses; some might do more than

A camera crew on *Campion* wait for an actor to emerge from the house. An actor must learn to ignore the welcoming committee!

we are doing, in terms of shooting a production, but students still have very little awareness when acting for the camera . . . One of the major complaints of our executives on the National Council for Drama Training (NCDT), in terms of accrediting courses, is the lack of camera training in our curricula. If you look at our employment schedules, you see just how television orientated our ex-students are. At least as much as theatre, and in some cases more. Television is often their first job when they come out, so it's quite clear there needs to be more training. It goes right back to the actual selection process: Do you take note of faces when you audition? Are you aware, when you are auditioning, that *that* face, or *that* body is in demand? That's where the real issue takes place, because if you don't look at them in this regard, and just look at them because they're clever actors with nice voices, and ignore those people with interesting faces, or interesting physicalities, or interesting personalities, who might not have particularly nice voices, you miss out. To me the incredible thing is the choice at the start. I see everybody on the recall, and I've taken people in because of their *look*. Whilst we can always change everything else, we can never change that! It depends how much value you put on the visuals. How much value do you put on that ability to communicate through the face, as well as through the voice? It isn't just the training, it's the *picking* of students. One of our most famous television stars is the perfect example: turned down at RADA and Central. Now I knew, that after spending three years here, he would never be a classic actor . . . but I could see his personality, and there aren't many like him, so we offered him a place immediately. That's the sort of decision I'm talking about.

M.T. Having picked the face, though, you then need to spend more time developing the technique, don't you?

Jago Yes. But what tends to happen in a lot of schools, is that they're all treated as though they're going to be classical actors. There *is* a value in that, but how much does it cost, training people to be the same? So, what you might see emerging is a streaming process, whereby everybody trains in all aspects, but some do more of a particular thing than others. For example, singing. We're having two concerts today; everybody takes part in the first concert, but those in the second might actually get jobs out of it!

I must say I liked Ralph Jago; his response to my questions was enthusiastic and direct and because he's aware of the inadequacies of the current camera training programme he's doing his best to do something about it.

Of course, many fine actors have never been to drama school, and there is no set route to success. Basically, if you are extremely talented, dedicated, and have the staying power, you stand as good a chance as any of entering the profession, but drama schools do provide a clearly defined path to follow, as well as entitling you to an Equity Union ticket on completion of the course (see Chapter 3). Personally I have absolutely no opinion as to who is offering the best training because I haven't done a survey beyond enquiring of the facilities on offer, but I have included a list of all the schools accredited by the NCDT in Appendix 1, and you should get as many brochures as possible. Try to get advice from people whose knowledge about such matters you trust, before coming to a decision. 'The Spotlight' advisory service (see page 34) may be able to offer you assistance in this direction too. But remember, just like schools and universities, the reputation of a drama college can vary from year to year. A particular school, for instance, may have attracted a well-known personality to its teaching ranks, or a fashionable movement teacher may be in current residence. Neither of these facts, however, may have any significant relevance to its overall ability to equip its students for the professional world ahead. Try to canvass the opinions of recent leavers if you get the opportunity. Another tip is to find out whether they regularly employ practising professionals, as well as their regular staff, as they often bring a whiff of fresh air to what can sometimes be a stuffy and complacent atmosphere.

Don't choose a school the way that I did. I was in my final year at a boarding school in Cumbria, all set to be a medic, when one of those 'Hello, I'm here to give you a chat on careers' chaps dropped by. He mentioned acting en passant, giving out the names of RADA, Central and Guildhall as 'suitable establishments in which to train'. I'd never heard of any of them; didn't even know one could *train* to be an actor, but fuelled by enthusiasm, I wrote off for all the audition applications. RADA's came first, so I sent my £1, travelled secretly to London (never been to the forbidden city before) 'got in', then broke the news to my shocked parents that I'd dropped one theatre in favour of another. As it happens I was lucky, I learned a lot, made a lifetime of friends, and thoroughly enjoyed myself, but I can't honestly suggest you take such an haphazard approach as I did!

One of the things you should take into account when deciding where to study is the school's location. It's not necessary to be in London all the time, but it's an advantage if your school has arrangements with a venue so that you can at least be seen in London in your final year. A 'Showcase' can be an important shop window for your talent, and agents and casting directors,

One of the things you should take into account when deciding where to study is the school's location

though often willing to visit, say the Fortune Theatre, where Bristol Old Vic hold their annual London bash, might not be so keen to troop off to Bristol to see what's on offer in one of their full productions. (I chose the words of my last sentence carefully, for as a young performer, you are very much 'on offer', and the ability to sell yourself should be an integral part of your weaponry.)

In America the twin centres for film/television and theatre production are Los Angeles and New York respectively (although many soaps are made in New York); it follows therefore that most training schools are to be found within their environs.

In the United Kingdom however, production and training centres are more diverse (Cardiff, Glasgow, Manchester and

Birmingham are important regional centres), though London remains the hub of the national wheel.

Most schools will have scholarships or bursaries on offer to qualifying students, but as far as council grants are concerned, local authorities only have to make statutory awards if you embark on a university degree course, and it can be quite difficult to get an award to attend drama school. Clearly, the better known establishment will influence a council's decision to some extent, but even so, if you are academically bright, you might think it best to opt for the safety of a university grant, which is mandatory.

Of course, unless you go in for a degree in drama (and even then your training won't be exclusively geared towards acting), you will have to forego the 'training' element a drama school affords, and settle for performance opportunities instead. But this might not be a bad thing. If you're good at English or History and enjoy your subjects, there's no earthly reason why you can't mentally settle for a thespian career eventually, while continuing your studies. Indeed this route can have positive financial advantages at the end of the day, for you may end up being able to practise a profession which could keep you in funds while looking for theatrical work. There are many private teachers (advertising widely in *The Stage* newspaper) who can help you improve your voice/movement/audition techniques if you can't attend full-time training – but again, seek advice or a recommendation before parting with your cash.

Although Oxford and Cambridge are well-known for their dramatic opportunities, they are by no means the only ones that have carved themselves a reputation in this direction. Hull, Manchester, York, Bristol and many others have fine records for developing thespian talent, and it's not necessary to pursue a degree in drama to have the opportunity to act either. It's up to you to make yourself known in whatever quarters you deem relevant. I always think that if you want something badly enough and have the talent to back it up, chances are you'll get it.

If, however, having completed a university degree course, you feel you would like to attend a full-time drama school for a while (it's not a bad idea, because you at least give yourself a chance to forget your previous orientation and acclimatise to a new), you will find that many drama schools offer post-graduate courses. They are usually shorter than their main (2–3 year) courses and take into account your broader experience of life.

Two or three months before you launch yourself on the unsuspecting public you must make sure that you have a decent set of photographs taken. Your drama school will no doubt advise you who to consider as a photographer, but you should also arm yourself with a copy of the current issue of *Contacts* (see Appendix 1) – it's updated every November and currently costs about £6 (+ £1 p&p) This little magazine contains just about every name, address and phone number you're ever likely to need as an actor, including more than 500 agents, as well as production companies and innumerable photographers. Have a look through the advertisements and decide which style of photograph you think suits you before making an expensive decision. Photographers' fees vary wildly; you can pay from £25 to £150 a session. A good tip is to get together with a couple of friends and negotiate a group rate, it will keep the price down. If the first photographer you try won't agree to do this, try another. Once you have your 'contact' sheet (some photographers will just give you the photo session and a 'contact' sheet, others will also agree to give you up to three 10 x 8 in prints as well), choose the ones that are most like you. Don't be tempted to pick the most glamourous pictures and don't go in for too many poses. You'll never need more than three – serious, happy, and interesting – and the chances are you'll find yourself falling in love with only one of them, which you'll use all the time.

You'll need a good photograph so that you can advertise yourself in the next issue of *The Spotlight*, a pictorial casting directory (one for actors and one for actresses), which is updated annually. (In America there are several equivalents of *The Spotlight* such as *The Players Guide*, *Academy Players Directory*, etc.) The directory used to offer different sized spaces at varying rates (full, half, quarter and eighth pages) but over the years they've done away with this system and nowadays the only space available is a half page. It is absolutely essential for you to find the money for this publication for it has world-wide circulation, and *The Spotlight* also put all their client's details on C.D. which is a computerised form of the directory giving more information plus photograph (this facility is used increasingly by potential employers) for no extra charge. These 'bibles' are issued annually, so don't be caught napping; anticipate your own arrival on the scene. The actors' edition of *The Spotlight* is published in April, so to be included you will need to have your application and new photograph with them by mid October. If you are simply renewing or updating your entry the deadline is November 1st. These dates remain constant every year. For the actresses' edition of *The Spotlight* the dates are mid April (new photos) and the beginning of May (renewal) for publication the following October. The charge (for 1994), including a photographic block, is £92.50p including VAT, or £86.50 for renewal. Although this may sound steep, it's actually very good value if you consider that the advertisement can save you a lot of money in the long run (instead of sending a snap every time you apply for a job, you can simply quote your *Spotlight* number). In addition, if you are a subscriber, *Spotlight* offers a casting advisory service. They will try to send representatives to see you in shows, and keep a record of up to ten of your acting credits. You should also keep them informed of your whereabouts as this can be useful if people are trying to contact you but don't know where you are. They will also advise you about the suitability of agents, and generally provide you with a focal point for any enquiries you may have. They are a very helpful and sympathetic bunch of people and subscription to their publication is therefore a 'must'.

At the same time that you are thinking about photographs you should also be thinking about getting a curriculum vitae (C.V.), or résumé, together. Although you may not have done anything other than drama school or university productions, it's important that you have one, if for no other reason than to let prospective employers and agents know the range of parts you usually play. It's also a good idea to incorporate a photograph into your C.V. so that there is a visual reference as well. Christopher Denys, the Principal of The Bristol Old Vic Theatre School has evolved a format for the students based on his years of experience as a director, 'All those photographs and bits of paper arriving on one's desk. At least everything is contained on one side of A4'. I agree with him. I don't think the layout can be bettered. It's clear, simple and informative. I should use something similar if I were you. Christopher Staines'

Christopher Staines

BRISTOL OLD VIC THEATRE SCHOOL

1/2 Downside Road
Clifton
Bristol BS8 2XF
(0272) 733535

3 Ridgeway Road
Farnham
Surrey GU9 8NN

Height:	5'10"
Eyes:	Brown
Hair:	Fair
Age:	23

New Actors Spotlight
Page 56

PROFESSIONAL

DIRECTOR

OBERON	*A Midsummer Night's Dream*	Shaun Macloughlin (BBC Radio)
PARTY GUEST	*Casualty*	Michael Brayshaw (BBC TV)
BOSSY	*Into The Magic Box*	Co devised (Oxford Theatre Company)

BRISTOL OLD VIC THEATRE SCHOOL

BOB CRATCHIT	*A Christmas Carol*	Christopher Denys
POMPEY	*Measure for Measure*	Andrew Hilton
SONNERIE	*Red Noses*	Elwyn Johnson
OCTAVIUS	*Man and Superman*	Nat Brenner
SIMON STIMSON	*Our Town*	Neil Rhoden

PRE TRAINING

Productions at Oxford University, Edinburgh Fringe and National Student Drama Festival.
Directed by David Farr, Theresa Heskins, Dominic Hill.

VALENTINE	*Two Gentlemen of Verona*
SWEENEY TODD	*Sweeney Todd (Sondheim)*
WOYZECK	*Woyzeck*
MALVOLIO	*Twelfth Night* - OUDS World Tour

SKILLS AND OTHER EXPERIENCE

Music - baritone ■ cello (grade VIII) ■ piano (grade VIII) ■ violin ■ clarinet
cabaret singer ■ pianist/MD ■ choirs ■ orchestras
junior exhibitioner at Royal Academy of Music
Dance - jazz ■ tap ■ basic ballet

- accents	- languages: German, French, Russian
- mime/mask skills	- BA (hons) English
- puppetry	- freelance editor/writer
- stage combat (intermediate)	- teacher of English as a foreign language
- gymnastics	- driving licence
- horse riding	- windsurfing

Chris Staines' C.V.

accomplishments, though exceptional in their diversity, reflect an increasing need for newcomers to be 'all-rounders'.

Once you have got all the details you want included in your C.V. together, have a few hundred of them printed. You should be able to find a printer who will do them for about £15 a hundred.

Duplicating them won't be significantly cheaper, and print quality is so much more professional. Invest in a good quality paper if you can afford it – we're all impressed by *looks* and *feel*, and this C.V. is your personal herald. If you follow this advice, you won't normally need to send out a photograph as well, which will save you a great deal of money.

If you budget for spending about £300 on photographs (get a few postcard 'repros' done for aunts, uncles and the odd fan – and have your name printed across the bottom), on advertising in *The Spotlight*, on printing your C.V., on buying envelopes and stamps, and on joining Equity, you will be on the right track. It would be a shame, if, having spent two or three years training, you failed to give yourself the launch you deserve.

Right. Time to talk briefly about Equity.

Chapter Three
Equity Entry

Although it is illegal for an employer to deny work to a non-union member, in practice, bona fide production companies will expect you to be a member of Equity. It's not so much that they are anxious to pay you as much money as possible, rather that membership of the union reassures them that they are employing a professional. It's important that you join as soon as possible, for Equity negotiates with employers to maintain minimum payments and conditions, and without their contracts, actors would receive even less money and be exploited even more than they are already.

In spite of Equity's efforts, we must appreciate that we live increasingly in a buyer's market, and union strength is not what it was. Minimum payments tend to be the going rate for the job. In times of recession, employers take fewer chances and scrabble among themselves to secure the services of 'bankable' names; there are fewer crumbs left on the table for the humble supporters. And it's getting worse.

You will see from the 'Equity Guide to Entry', which I quote in full in Appendix 2, that there is no provision for young actors without previous experience to seek employment directly in film and television. They must first 'qualify' with provisional membership. I'm sure this ruling has been arrived at because, historically, actors tended to go into rep, learn their craft, and then seek work in the more lucrative areas of television or the West End. But times have changed rapidly and dramatically. There simply isn't the volume of work available in provincial theatre anymore to absorb the constant flow of newcomers, and while 'television' work, in all sorts of video guises, permeates into every nook and cranny of our lives, the theatre continues to contract to such an extent that, for most young professionals, the only hope of getting seen or fulfilling acting ambitions

is to work in a profit-sharing enterprise (fat chance of profit) in the upstairs room of a bar, or the crypt of a local church.

Not only is this condition of entry out-dated but it positively discriminates against actors who may be only really suited to working in the media. We get back to the 'think theatre' syndrome again.

The Americans have two separate unions, Equity, for theatre work, and the Screen Actors Guild (SAG) for . . . well, screen actors! Now we certainly don't want two negotiating bodies, but we must surely recognize that actors need to have all the roads open, as they do in the States. To join SAG, for instance, all you need is a contract for a minimum of three days work and the ability to pay $1012.50 ($970 joining fee and the first annual subscription of $42.50).

Notwithstanding union guidelines, if a producer wants you to appear in his next film and you have not yet 'qualified', all he has to do is state his case to Equity, and you'll be given a contract. After all, it's illegal to deny people the opportunity to work. The trouble is, while Equity still talks about 'provisional membership' and 'qualifying periods', it's unlikely that either you or your agent will have the temerity to suggest you for any screen roles, and you may well remain idle.

Although graduates from accredited schools may seek employment in the media, there are exclusion clauses pertaining to West End and National Theatre employment. In my opinion, and I know many hard-pressed actors will disagree with me, I don't think the union should be in the business of protectionism – for that's what these clauses amount to. Some actors will make a career from their craft and some actor's won't, and I can't see why obstacles should be put in anyone's path. Life's difficult enough as it is.

Perhaps, in the not too distant future an enlightened Equity Council will abandon quotas and qualifying periods, encourage extras to join, to add to its sorely stretched resources, concentrate on improving conditions and the rates of pay, and make no distinction between its members. The full guide to equity appears on page 135, as does the address of the Screen Actors Guild (SAG).

Chapter Four
Actors' Agents

A popular fallacy, which must be dealt with straight away, is that once you have an agent there's no looking back. Wrong. Agents can be extremely useful to you, providing they have enough of the right contacts and keep their ears close to the ground. They can also open doors to young actors, by way of introductions to casting directors, who may not have immediate need of their services, but might remember them for future reference.

Because most casting directors make the bulk of their living from casting commercials, which have a quick turnround (they are often casting several at once), it's absolutely essential that you are known to as many of them as possible. All agents, worthy of the name, will number several casting directors (as well as directors and producers, who may also be on their 'books') among their personal friends. It's important for both casting director and agent to forge these links as they need each other; most will spend many off-duty hours socialising in each other's company, and it's good news for you if you find an engaging, gregarious agent.

It's impossible to advise you whether you should look for a large or a small agent, as both have their virtues. The larger agents, with many top people on their books, may well have the opportunity to introduce your name into a conversation, as a supporting player, while discussing the availability of their most wanted star. On the other hand, they may not have the time to find you some good repertory work, while a smaller, more personal agent may.

By and large I suppose it's fair to say that the more 'high powered' your agent is, the more likely you are to be either catapulted to the front of your profession comparatively quickly, or be forgotten with equal speed. So don't get overly

impressed by posh notepaper, accents and addresses. Yes, you might want to take a gamble with a high-flier, but on the other hand you might want to work at your craft slowly and receive some good solid support from an agent who isn't going to be pre-occupied with wet-nursing his stars for much of his working day. There's only a finite number of hours in which to do business, so try to ensure you'll get a few minutes of your agent's attention every now and then.

It's worth reminding you again that there are more than five hundred agents listed in *Contacts*. Most are one-man bands or small partnerships, and you will need to find one you feel comfortable with. It's no good going with an agent you think looks shifty, speaks badly, and is scruffily dressed. If that's what *you* think, what sort of impression do you think he will make on potential employers? Exactly. During my time working in television I can't tell you the number of times I've heard casting directors groan when they hear their assistants say, (hand carefully cupping the mouthpiece) 'It's So and So on the line. Wants to know if she can make a few suggestions?' They usually feign

to be in meetings, are out, or are away on holiday – anything, in fact, to get away from 'that terrible woman' – or man, I hasten to add. Finding work is difficult enough, without having an unhelpful agent, so don't rush into anything.

Try to find someone who has a friendly secretary, with a pleasant telephone manner, for they are the first port of call for any ships that may be coming in.

I talked to Roger Carey, principal partner of Roger Carey Associates, who describes his agency as 'medium-sized'. He also represents some directors and producers and therefore is in a position to suggest his actors to them when they are casting. As he has been in the business for twenty-five years, I thought I would ask him a few questions on your behalf.

I asked him how he kept abreast of new talent entering the business.

Carey Through drama schools and fringe theatre. I cover as many fringe shows as I can, but I mostly keep abreast of new talent through drama schools, especially accredited ones. Most of them advise their students not to select agents until they've graduated. Talk to agents by all means, but don't do any selecting until you've left.

M.T. Why's that?

Carey Because a lot of very good agents won't bother covering drama schools, particularly the provincial ones; but they *will* cover final showcases in London. It wouldn't be wise, therefore, to sign up until everyone's had a chance to see you.

There is a problem with the big agents just covering showcases, however. They might just turn up and flaunt their twenty named clients in front of the students, who will be impressed. That's what happened last year with the Bristol students, where at least three of them were already covered by good agents, but hadn't yet been 'taken up'. And when I discovered that they'd joined (Mrs Big), I asked one of them, 'Why?', and he replied, 'Because of her list'. I said, 'Well, one swallow doesn't make a summer', and he said that they had all been very impressed with her list of clients. She has the clout to pick up the phone to a casting director, because of the various names she represents, and say, 'I've just taken on a wonderful new young actor, and I think you should meet him.' A smaller agent may find it very difficult to make this sort of direct introduction. But the smaller agent may work much harder trying to map out an actor's career than a larger one. It's not all about high-powered introductions. I think students sometimes join agents for the wrong reasons, I really do.

M.T. Do you sign actors up to a contract?

Carey No, we don't. People did 'sign' actors, and directors too, but that's stopped. In America, every one who joins an agent is signed, but that's not the case here.

M.T. So what you're saying is, although an actor may have been 'taken up' by (Mrs Big), because they're not 'signed', they could technically change their mind and find someone else?

Carey They could do, yes, but that rarely happens. What *does* happen sometimes, is that a very good young student might leave drama school and be 'courted' by somebody who will try and impress their potential client; will phone up casting directors and ask the student to go and meet them, and whilst the actor will, of course, say 'yes', they still haven't committed themselves to that agent. The client will be able to do any job that this potential agent has set up, and still be able to go with someone else they might meet subsequently and like better. And this does happen.

The relationship between actors and agents has changed now. Once upon a time, agents used to sit down and say, 'yes, my office would love to represent you', but now sometimes we're told to wait for a decision – so we, as agents, are having to audition and jockey for position.

M.T. In my day, it was *always* the agent who picked the actors, not vice versa . . .

Carey Absolutely.

M.T. . . . but when the situation is reversed what criteria you use when deciding whether or not to take on an actor?

Carey Well, I usually try and see them in their last year at drama school. I try and watch the last three shows, not just the showcase production . . .

M.T. But not only you . . . most of the good agents are chasing the same people . . .

Carey Yes. If not *all* of the good agents – it's like bees round a honey pot. So often the smaller agents lose out, even if they've followed this particular student throughout their last year. The student, as I've said before, is going to be impressed by the bigger agents with the more impressive client list. This used to be particularly true only of RADA, but now it's also true of most of the others.

M.T. But what about the actors who aren't considered to be the bees knees? How do they set about getting an agent?

Carey It's very sad . . . in the sense that the 'choice students', as it were, are given most of the best roles in the showcase production, and often also throughout the year . . . and some very good actors, just because they don't look like Greek gods and are not dazzlingly beautiful, are playing men of seventy-five.

Now, I remember years ago at RADA this happened to a young man called Jonathan Hyde, who was in the same year as Ben Cross, who was snapped up. Nobody took much notice of Jonathan because he was playing an old man, and only one agent approached him. Jonathan Hyde flew! Ben Cross went on to do *Chariots of Fire*, but Jonathan Hyde did more work than Ben over the next two years. This, of course, is also an example of how principals at drama schools some-times, unfortunately, favour certain students.

M.T. But for every star student, there must be another dozen who aren't. How do those who are not the chosen few set about getting an agent?

Carey There are hundreds of agents. Everybody, today, wants one. It's far more important than it used to be. Most students now tend to think, 'once I've got an agent, then I'll get work'. It doesn't work like that. Having an agent is not a passport to success. When I lectured at LAMDA, as an agent, I tried to

stress the importance of looking for work yourself, as an actor, and *then* getting a good agent to come and see you. But because everyone is so preoccupied with getting an agent, *any agent*, many students are going with terrible ones, and I think that's wrong. They should be told, and hopefully a book like this will help them. Merely 'getting an agent' doesn't mean you'll get continuous work – it might mean you get forgotten about.

M.T. Now, suppose you've got a young actor on your books that you've got a lot of faith in, who's terribly broke, do you ever consider giving him an advance?

Carey No. I'd love to, but I'm not a philanthropic society, I can't.

M.T. Do any of the agents, do you think?

Carey I don't think they do today.

M.T. But you might consider giving an actor an advance against a fee you know is definitely coming in.

Carey Yes, I might, but we're not allowed to, by rights . . .

M.T. By what rights?

Carey By the Employment Agencys Act. As the sum of money comes in for an actor, the agent takes his 10% business charge, and the rest goes to the actor. The agent can't take money from his client's account; he can't start advancing money out of his business account either, because he has running costs – unless he's a very wealthy agent. But even so, I can't see it happening today. It might happen with established actors, doing films and television series, who make fifty, sixty, seventy thousand pounds a year, but you don't know the nature of the beast where a young actor is concerned – or whether the actor is even going to stay with you!

M.T. How would you describe yourself as an agent?

Carey About ten years ago, I'd use the words 'Personal Management'. I used to represent about twenty or thirty actors, but nowadays we have to represent more than that because we have to pay our bills; actors' fees on which, of course, our income is based, have not risen in line with our costs. We have to represent more actors today because we have to pay our bills. Most people carry, I would say, fifty to a hundred people on their books, unless you have some very established names, such as John Alderton, Pauline Collins, Peter Egan, Vanessa Redgrave . . . and then you're sitting in a white palace with maybe only thirty clients.

   I think I would consider myself one of the top twenty, but I'm still a medium-sized agent. I'm not talking about organisations like (he mentions some) which I see as sausage factories – facility houses for the Americans in this country, really.

M.T. What is the ratio of men to women amongst your clients?

Carey If I look after sixty actors; I would say about forty men to twenty women.

M.T. How do you keep a balance between the different types of actors you've got on your books?

Carey Well, I suppose I carry more actors between the ages of twenty to forty than the forty to sixty age group, and the sixty plusses. We carry very few seventeen to twenty year olds, but I've got a feeling this will change in the next five years.

M.T. How effective do you think agents are in negotiating salaries for actors in these days of finite production budgets?

Carey If one of my actors, a student who I'd just taken on, say, came to me and said, 'look, I've got this theatre job, and they want to talk to me about money, could you help?', I *know* that if I negotiate I will earn my 10%, because I know I can raise the offer by more than 10%.

M.T. But very often, budgets are based on the minimum and they can't be shifted from that, and it's a question of take it or leave it, isn't it?

Carey Yes, it is, but I personally have never had to deal with the minimum, so I can't answer that question. There has never been a time when I haven't been able to earn my percentage, otherwise I wouldn't be able to do it. If it did come to it, of course, one would have to do the job and manage with the minimum company wage offered. And if it was a student, then I wouldn't take a percentage.

M.T. What sort of fees can a young actor expect from a television appearance, say, in an episode of a series?

Carey Well, they've stopped paying episode fees at the BBC. Now they pay a weekly fee. I think a newcomer, maybe, doing an episode of *EastEnders*, or even two episodes, might get £450–£500 a week.

M.T. More for ITV?

Carey It depends. If it's *Emmerdale Farm*, you might get £350, but you're paid by the episode at ITV, so they might, on a long running contract with an actor, if they want him for, say, six months, decide to pay him £350 an episode, and guarantee him 24 episodes over six months, which is one a week. But the chances are, he's going to do more than one episode a week.

M.T. So what would he be likely to average on, weekly?

Carey You have to take it on the length of the engagement, really. If his contractual obligation is something like six months, with the guarantee of an episode a week at £350, he might get more than one episode a week, perhaps two, so end up getting £700. That's a newcomer. The downside of that is that he might only get £300 a week, but if he does two episodes, he still comes out with £600, plus rehearsals and production days, of course.

M.T. What about the daily rate for films, such as they are in this country?

Carey You might get £600–£700 a week. On a day, you might get maybe £300–£400.

M.T. What's your commission rate?

Carey It varies with different agents. With us it's 10% for television, films, radio and reperatory theatre, 15% on commercials and voice–overs; 15% on repeats and residuals – it may sound a lot, but we have to mop up some sort of deficit in terms of couriers and faxes when chasing the money, and with repeats and residuals the actor himself is not actually having to work for the money again. Then there's personal appearances: I represent quite a few regulars from television series, and if they make celebrity appearances – say open a shopping centre or a bar – I will take 15%. If I negotiate a magazine or newspaper article I also take 15% on that.

M.T. So it's really 15% for 'extra' activities?

Carey Absolutely, but the main thrust of the industry – television, film, rep and radio, is 10%.

M.T. Would you take commission from a young actor getting a job at minimum salary in rep?

Carey If he's on a six month contract I'm afraid I'll have to, because that means I'll have an actor lost off my books for six months, not earning. And meanwhile, as he's a young actor, I've probably already spent quite a lot of money moving him around – trying to get people to meet him, writing introductory letters, biking and faxing stuff to people – even postage can cost several hundred pounds. I don't think it's therefore greedy of me to ask for my 10%, so I can keep my doors open!

M.T. But if it was a short engagement and the actor was broke?

Carey Well, what I have done in the past, where a new young actor in the business is not a schedule D client, (pays tax annually based on past earnings) and they have to pay PAYE, I have taken 10% of whatever they come away with, and not 10% on the figure I actually negotiated.

M.T. Should actors keep in regular touch with you, when they're unemployed?

Carey Yes, I think once a week; just to check and say hello. It's also psychologically good for the actor, because I am the link between them and the business.

M.T. Do you ever sack actors from your list?

Carey Oh yes, frequently.

M.T. Why?

Carey It's not to do with talent, it's to do with everything else. If, for example, the agency is not working for the actor, we might suggest they find a fresh voice. Sometimes, it's time for an actor to move on if confidence goes out of the relationship between the actor and the agent; the actor says things like, 'Are you sure you're talking to the right people?', 'All my friends are getting to meet people, why aren't I', 'Do you know so and so?', treating me like . . . I think then it's time to end the partnership. I mean, what's the point in representing someone who's unhappy?

And don't forget that actors can sack agents as well as vice versa. It can be far more underhand, as well, in the sense that they can be scouting round for other agents behind your back, while you're still working on their behalf. Sometimes, an actor turns round to an agent and says, 'I'm leaving you, because I got the last three jobs myself'. As an agent, I stress to my clients that they get *all* the jobs, if you see what I mean, by virtue of themselves, but they need me there to play good cop/bad cop, to hustle and sell them, and tell the business how wonderful they are, etc. It's embarrassing for an actor to have to do that himself, we agents do that, and let the actor get on with his work.

M.T. Do you have any tie-ups for representation in other countries?

Carey Yes, in America.

M.T. So that means that you would split your commission with another agent in America?

Carey Yes. If I find a client of mine in this country work in America or anywhere in the world *myself*, then I will take my 10% completely, and not share it. If my American contact agent finds my English client a job, whether he's shooting here or in America, *he* will negotiate the deal through me, but he will be negotiating the deal and talk on behalf of my client as though he was the agent, and we would then split the commission.

M.T. What about representation in the rest of Europe, as more and more co-production deals are coming into being?

Carey I don't find it that important at the moment. I have points of contact in Europe, and I use them if I need to. But the clients that I represent tend to come to me when they work in Europe, so there's no need for me to put the negotiation through another agent. If I find that my client is going to spend a lot of time abroad filming, then of course I'm willing to share a commission with someone who will sit there and look after them.

M.T. How much of a personal interest do you take in your clients, or is it strictly business?

Carey Oh no. I have a great personal interest in my clients. It's a marriage. We're not dealing with potatoes and peas in this business, we're dealing with human beings, and it's terribly important that one gets one's priorities right. Personal interest is very, very important.

M.T. Finally, what state do you think the business will be in in the next few years? Will it improve?

Carey Yes, I hope so. I think America is creeping out of recession and we are showing signs of it. I just hope to God that we begin to make a lot more films than we have been recently . . . but anyway the indications are that things will improve. At least that's what the casting directors are saying . . .

I am very grateful to Roger Carey for taking the time to give me such a useful and informative interview, and I am delighted he can always raise an actors salary by more than the 10% he charges, and that he never has to deal with minimum fees. He is exceptionally fortunate.

Chapter Five
Casting Considerations

Casting directors are employed either by advertising agencies, film or television companies, or sometimes, by individual producers and directors to find them suitable actors for their productions. Depending on the brief from their client they can either produce a wide range of actors of differing physical attributes but the same 'appeal', i.e. winsome, cute, jolly, sad-looking, or a narrow one consisting of actors who need to be of a certain height, age or build. To do their job properly they naturally have to know a great number of actors and, more importantly to be able to assess their abilities, qualities and facial appeal.

Although casting directors don't, themselves, make final decisions they can be very persuasive if they feel an actor is right for a part and the director is a ditherer. Don't prostrate yourself before them – or worse, get involved emotionally with one in the hope that it will produce work (because it usually doesn't) but on the other hand do try to present the nicer aspects of your personality.

Gill Titchmarsh is a friendly, efficient, extremely tidy person, who works from the airy ground floor office of her house in West London. She has been a casting director for twenty-six years, six of which were spent working in the United States, and has a very broad experience of working 'across the board' – from constant television commercials (Ford, Halifax, Fosters, etc.), from which she earns the bulk of her living, to films and series, (the recent children's feature, *Dragon World*, Lynda La Plante's *Seekers*) which tend to be more thinly spread throughout the year.

While she was in the States she found she was often rung by visiting English directors, who needed 'English looking' actors for their American shoots, and found it an enormous challenge to get to know not only a whole lot of new faces, but an entirely different media 'culture' to that which she had been used to. You can imagine her surprise on returning to the United Kingdom to find that the television industry she once knew so well had totally changed. She was particularly taken aback to find such a plethora of production companies and the increasing use of video as a teaching and information tool.

One of her most important tasks was to acquaint herself with all the new talent that had emerged in her absence. A casting director operates much like an actor's agent – except that they are buying, as opposed to selling. Nevertheless the actor is the commodity that is at the centre of the deal, and I was keen to hear what Gill had to say. I asked her, if, like Roger Carey, she scouted the drama schools. 'Well I like to try and catch the third years. I don't break my neck to go to the provinces but some of them do bring their showcases to London'. I asked her what schools she covered in London – 'Webber Douglas, LAMDA, sometimes Central and RADA. The standard varies; you have good years and bad years. At the moment the Bristol Old Vic has a consistently high standard. It seems to be one school that gives them a completely rounded education in theatre; they also emphasise the importance of television and film technique. They still don't cover agents, or casting directors, though really I've never understood why. I'm sure they don't invite enough people to talk to the students in their final year to tell them what to prepare for, but of all the students coming out of drama schools theirs are the most preferred of all'. I couldn't let her get away with that one without a protestation. 'This year!', I added, 'Don't let's get carried away; when I was at RADA it was THE place to be; mind you Albert Finney being there helped . . . a couple of years later RADA was out and Central was in, and so it goes on . . .

Let's change the subject for a minute and talk about the States; I've never had the opportunity to talk to someone with first hand experience of casting over there. Is it very different?

Gill Well casting in the States is very much film orientated, unless you're in Chicago or New York, and actors are less well schooled in drama. They need a good director, many of them, otherwise they get flat . . . give uninteresting performances, as you most probably have seen.

M.T. What about the approach of actors in the States and the approach of English actors? And please be honest.

Gill Well there is an enormous gap, because in America they think their country is wonderful and they love each other, and they're very hospitable and this runs right through everything in their lives. So the actors don't care what they do providing they can keep afloat. Every cafe in L.A. has writers and certainly actors, waiting on tables. Actors out there are quite remarkable, they would spend their last cent on decent photographs, presentation . . . it's very important to keep your head down and really go for what you want, and not just slop your way along. It takes application. I sometimes feel that there isn't the same dedication here . . . There's other differences of organisation too. In the States if you want to do commercials you have to have a commercial agent; if you do theatre you have a theatrical agent, and you have a manager as well, and the theatrical agent also handles you for film. But sometimes you might even have another agent as well, so you're paying an enormous amount of commission to all these agents and managers and things.

M.T. So what percentage of your salary goes on commissions?

Gill I would say anything up to thirty percent, by the time you've dished out to various agents. Commission rates tend to vary much more than over here.

M.T. But fees, particularly in films and television are much higher aren't they?

Gill Well not necessarily. Obviously it's a bigger country so you have to take that into consideration.
   In America actors work to the SAG, that's the Screen Actors Guild, minimum, and actors up to a certain level . . . and I mean reasonable actors, just get the minimum. Anyone who's got a telly series, a 'soap' or something like that, would be over scale . . . as well as established actors from New York or Chicago. In Hollywood the quality of acting isn't usually as good. That's why a lot of the actors come out to L.A. from

New York and Chicago during the pilot season when they're booking all the 'soaps' and things . . . What was I saying? Ah yes, fees.

For films and television the S.A.G. minimum is currently about $480 a day or $1,700 a week . . . something like that. So all the actors on S.A.G. scale do the work for that amount as their basic fee, their studio fee. Then there's extras for hairdressing and wardrobe calls, that sort of thing. In commercials I think the minimum is just over $400 a day for principals, then extras for this and that. With use fees you can earn $25,000 from a McDonald's commercial for example, which is networked.

M.T. How does that compare to English commercials rates?

Gill On a £200 studio fee, for the day . . . well, say, £250, I think they could earn . . . say, anything between £4000–£5000. On one that goes out a lot, say again a McDonald's commercial here, or one for a washing powder, which is shown up and down the country, and really does get plugged they can earn a lot more.

M.T. So an ordinary actor, on say a basic studio fee of £250, plus repeats – if it's a successful commercial shown in lots of areas, could earn about £11,000?

Gill Could do. I did do a well-known washing powder, and they really plugged it, and that actor earned £30,000.

M.T. On a studio fee of £250? That's a lot of money!

Gill Not bad, is it?

M.T. In America they go in for a lot more typecasting than we do don't they?

Gill There's a lot of typecasting here though for commercials. Mind you I see a lot of our better actors playing many different roles. There's more chance here, if you're really good, to play, say really glamorous people one minute, and the next be frightfully unglamorous in, say, *The Bill*. So actors here do get a chance to do that sort of crossover.

M.T. Tell me, do actors tend to write directly to you for work, or are you mostly dealing with agents?

Gill I get approaches from both actors and agents, but I think most actors know you can't necessarily rely on an agent to really work hard for you. They're very good at picking up a phone when a casting director phones in, but they're not that good at doing mass mail outs on your behalf, because its expensive, so a lot of actors do it themselves.

M.T. Do you see actors if you like the photographs they send in?

Gill Oh yes. I get a 'sense'. I used to be a photographer's assistant and I have an ability to pick out the best actor for the job from a bunch of twelve purely by his photograph . . . of course if someone is brilliant, but he's got a lousy, lousy photograph I might pass him by. But generally that photograph 'speaks' an awful lot; the look in the eye is the most important thing I think.

M.T. And what about agents . . . I mean, do you have a certain number of agents you phone when you're casting and ask them if they've got anybody suitable? Is it a sort of Gill Titchmarsh repertory company of agents?

Gill No. There's a sort of scale of good agents, but it depends what you're casting, because some agents specialise in young people or old people or a mixture . . . a good set of mediocre actors . . . or beautiful people, so, as you're on the phone all the time, you know which of the agents to call when you get a brief in . . . who to attack first so to speak, and then if you've got a lot of characters to cast, you might run all the characters through the agents. There are some agents you really respect. But a lot of agents will suggest people who are totally wrong, and there are very few agents that you can actually trust.

M.T. So, *you* know, because of your experience, which agents to trust, and which agents are likely to provide you with the people you want in any category, but how does a young actor, just coming into the business? How should he, in your opinion, set about looking for an agent to represent him?

Gill Well, he can buy *Contacts*, in which he will be faced with about five or six pages of agents names.

M.T. But it doesn't tell you anything about their quality.

Gill No, it doesn't tell you anything about them at all. So the next stage is to make an appointment with *The Spotlight*. There are a couple of people there who will sit down and spend time with an actor, get to know them a little bit, and point them in the right direction. There's been a wealth of actors' co-operatives, which are agencies run by the actors themselves, and some are doing quite well, but a lot of them aren't because they don't know how to sell people, or the people they are selling aren't terribly good in the first place. I had an actor in this morning, he trained over here and then went on to the States and Canada . . . came back here, and hasn't worked for four years. He's got hair down to 'here' (indicating her knees), looks like a Red Indian and is so limited because of a) his appearance, and b) his acting ability; his voice is so awful that I didn't know what to say. I mean what can I tell an actor like that? I pointed him in the direction of 'Uglies Agency' where he could earn some money as an 'extra'. You never know, he might get 'picked up' in the studio if he works as an 'extra' and given some more to do.

M.T. It's all about 'looks' isn't it? If actors know the part they are being interviewed for, and they usually do, should they come looking as near to that character as they possibly can?

Gill Yes. If an actor comes in to see a director and he *becomes* the character he's more likely to get the part. But so many actors come in, having been given the script out in reception, and instead of thinking about the character they're to be in five minutes time, they're much happier chatting to someone they haven't seen for ten years. Then their name is called and 'Whoops!' they grab the script . . . At the preliminary casting I would have sat him down and said 'This is your character, expect this, expect that, the director will want to play it this way or that way . . .' and he says 'Yes, yes, yes' . . . take him in and the director says 'Do you know anything about this character?' and he says 'No'! . . . they don't listen!

They should, a) make sure that they have the script, b) don't come in and sit down like 'lemons', and, c) If there's nobody around they should ask someone, *somewhere*, for a script – so they can start to prepare for the casting. So many actors come in; they start performing at the beginning of the dialogue, finish it, and then cut off. So if they've created a mood during the piece, they ruin it as soon as they've finished the last word – bang, straight back to 'Joe Bloggs'. Whereas if they'd just given it a little bit of thought, and given the character a slight beginning and end . . . the mood, you know . . . to whatever piece they're reading, even if its only for a commercial, it just makes me, as an audience, get more involved with the character. It makes the director say 'Hey, he *is* that character!' But so many don't do it! They come in, they're nervous, they don't think; they don't use their brains.

M.T. So it's confidence really, that's what it comes down to, confidence and concentration at a casting session.

Gill Yes, but they should also be 'aware' . . . When I was in the States I used to be invited to acting courses as a special guest, and I used to take along scripts with me and give the actors bits to learn and then watch them play them out . . . and they just . . . you know sometimes if you talk to an actor 'one to one', you realise how totally and utterly naive they can be! There are some actors who are natural performers, and just instinctively know what's expected . . . and directors just gravitate to them because they know they're not going to have trouble on the set; they don't want actors who are moody, or worried about their hair! . . . Some actors come in and the first thing they say is 'Now when are you shooting? I'll see if I'm free!' . . . I mean, the director immediately thinks 'They're going to be trouble!' . . . and he's probably right with that attitude . . . no sense of timing. Actors can be their own worst enemies. On the other hand, sometimes they have hold of the wrong end of the stick and don't know what on earth they're doing at the session because they haven't got the right information about a part. All too often very little information gets passed on to the actor.

Take commercials for example; the agent should get the right information from the casting director in order to tell the actor what character they're coming in for. Men are generally good about coming in a suit or a jacket if they're told to. Women I can tell to wear high heels, nice make-up, nice hair, . . . and they come in jeans and no make-up, and the casting director says 'Didn't you get the brief?' Because the tapes of the casting session are sent off to the client who may be in Italy or somewhere, and he is expecting to see something that is in the area of what he's casting.

M.T. I suppose these days, casting, particularly for commercials, is done, as you've said, at long distance. The person who is ultimately going to make the decision often does so purely on the evidence of the tape he's sent.

Gill Absolutely. Once an interview has been taped it can't be edited, and actors don't have a second chance. Because of the EC a vast amount of work is generated from other European countries. English actors are very popular and well-liked on the Continent, and the employers get extremely good value for their money. I hope that continues. . .

Chapter Six
Soaps and Such

Soap operas, so called because these domestic adventures were sponsored by soap manufacturers in the United States after the Second World War, are the largest employers of actors these days. Indeed it's hard to find a drama on television that doesn't fall into this category, whatever its producers might say. Their range is enormous. Posh (expensive), filmed 'soaps' in the *Dynasty* mould tend to run in a series, of say thirteen weeks, to match the Spring, Summer, Autumn or Winter schedules. But it's the twice or thrice weekly 'soaps' that really hook an audience.

There tends to be much more dialogue and less action in these operas than any other screened drama, and the camera tends to focus more on close-ups. This is due partly to the fact that the regular domestic sets (and I include pubs, police stations, shops and offices, etc.) in which they revolve are singularly uninteresting visually, but more importantly it is because there is a good deal of narrated action – 'You'll never guess what happened to Susan last night' (followed by a graphic description). So the action is *dialogue* led. Next time you watch such a programme, if you close your eyes you will find it's not usually difficult to follow what's going on. Quite often I find myself thinking that some programmes would be best served on radio!

The first time you 'go on the floor' (set foot in the studio) of a serial you have often seen on television, you will be amazed how small all the sets look; hardly room to swing a cat very often. This is because the cameras are usually too close to the subjects they are shooting (lack of space) to create an image that reflects the true perspective of what they are shooting. A true perspective for the human eye, that is. Our normal, focused vision is about twenty-four degrees, and in order to encapsulate all the action in a scene, a camera may have to open its iris to fifty degrees, which, when transmitted and viewed on a small screen is well within our sharp focus range. So what is in fact a small room can *appear* to be twice as large as it is in reality. Because of the distort created by the use of such a wide lens, you may often notice the verticals of a set appear to bend.

If a room appears to be larger than it is, it follows that the distance between objects often appears to be greater than it is too. This can have repercussions for the actors. As human beings we have a natural, comfortable, distance between us when we talk to each other. We've all experienced a sense of discomfort if someone gets unnaturally close, and tend to back off a little. Very often the director will rehearse a two-handed scene perfectly naturally in the rehearsal room, but when the scene gets transposed to the studio he will ask you to 'get closer together'. This is because the camera is unable to include the two of you from the position it is shooting from; perhaps it can not be repositioned for lack of space. From the director's vantage point in the gallery (the control room where the director and technicians oversee the proceedings) it will seem that there is an acre of space between you, whereas in actual fact you are virtually sitting in each other's laps. I've often been amazed, when I've set up a scene in the gallery and then gone on to the floor to check a few things, at this visual deception. The answer is, I'm afraid, to get used to acting with your space invaded. It won't look odd to the viewer, even though you might not be able to believe it at the time.

You will also find that often scenes will start with some fairly inconsequential dialogue (as you come into a pub for instance) and that the 'meat' of the scene starts when you get to the bar counter. Timing your walk is therefore crucial. You can save yourself a lot of time by starting at the bar and saying the lines in reverse while walking out of the pub. This will tell you how long it takes to say the lines at the speed you intend to walk, and the point in the dialogue you need to appear in vision through the door, to enable you to get to the right spot in time for your important line.

You can equate 'soap operas' to the manufactured product that used to sponsor them. The schedules are carefully honed production machines, designed to get the most 'bars' out of the system, for the minimum expenditure of cash and resources. Actors are the ingredient that provides the lather. And the more you know about the manufacturing process, the better you will be equipped to cope with it.

Most shows in England (though America is fast following suit) are videotaped, and include a mixture of location and studio material. (*Casualty* and *Emmerdale Farm* have more location than *Coronation Street*, for example, because they are more action based). They also usually incorporate a short rehearsal period. *The Bill* is the exception to this generality, for it is shot entirely on location, with no prior rehearsal, in and around London.

Mike Dormer, one of the *The Bill's* producers, kindly put me in the picture. 'There are three single camera production units, Red, Blue and Green. Each has its own producer and director, and each episode is shot in five days (anything from 33–55 scenes). Regular actors may be invloved in three episodes at any one time and have to 'flit' between units.'

Consequently the only rehearsals the actors get is when they are setting up for a shot. This, however, is not as bad as it sounds, and no different than any fast film shoot. The communication skills of the director determine the ease and confidence with which an actor plays a scene and Mike was at pains to assure me that the performances were the cornerstone of the series – even if it sometimes meant ditching shooting niceties in order to keep an episode within the schedule.

Mike also had a very helpful tip for visiting actors, 'The series is police driven, so it's important for guests to remember it's their reaction to the police that gives us the drama. Sometimes there are expections to this rule, but when visiting artists take the lead it's obvious from the script.'

Listen and react, then, is the usual order of the day.

Coronation Street and *EastEnders* are fairly representative of both ends of the spectrum as far as an actor's schedule is concerned, and it's worth taking a closer look at them.

EastEnders is the more complicated of the two because they alternate between their three episodes, recording their outside scenes in different weeks from their studio shoot, whereas *Coronation Street* encompasses their entire location and studio input within the space of a single week. If you are working on

'Lie still while I shoot you'. Christopher Ellison struggles to regain his composure in *The Bill*

EastEnders you might have to have six episodes floating around in your head at the same time, if you are a regular character. Actors, however, develop a facility for coping with this, and bits of paper containing the lines of the relevant episodes are often to be seen popping out of their various pockets – like moths! Personally I would advise you to get a very thorough understanding of the way you intend to play a character (so that his or her actions, and more importantly *re*actions become second nature) and then concentrate on learning the lines you need to deliver for your next encounter with the camera. In other words

The cast of *EastEnders* rehearse a sing-song round the piano on the set of the Queen Vic

KEEP IT SIMPLE. If you spend your energies concentrating on what has to be done today, tomorrow will take care of itself. Don't clutter your head with imaginery problems – deal with them as and when they appear. Don't bother, either being too pedantic when working out moves in an internal rehearsal situation for an exterior scene, because everything will look and feel different when you actually get on to the 'back lot' (literally an exterior complex at the back of the studios where Albert Square and its environs stand). Directors can be just as guilty of time wasting in this respect, and many is the time when, as an actor, I've been pulled up for 'walking through a wall', I've had to bite my tongue from saying 'Of course I won't walk through it when it's there, you wally.'

Leonard Lewis is the Executive Producer of *EastEnders*, and I asked him how young actors and actresses might set about getting a part in the show. He paused for thought before he replied, 'Difficult isn't it? Because there aren't that many opportunities. But we work these days very much through casting advisers . . . we have a very good one. We rely on her to supply people for interviews, rather than in the old days when the directors used to look for people themselves, didn't they? But these days it's very much done through the casting department.'

M.T. So she'd be in touch with the agents?

Lewis Yes. And she goes and does a lot of looking about. So it's worth young actors making contact with casting directors.

M.T. Do you have a casting advisor specifically for *EastEnders*?

Lewis (Beat) We .. ll, yes but that's likely to change as time goes by. I think the general rule is that they should be looking to get known by as many casting advisors and casting directors as they can . . . as well as by directors.

M.T. Could they approach directors and producers themselves if they haven't got an agent?

Lewis Well, I'll tell you what happens. If an actor writes to me, unless it's someone I know, I pass it straight on to my casting adviser . . . I might acknowledge it but that's about all. With someone I know it's different.

M.T. And what about being a regular in the show, who's involved in that choice?

Lewis That's the producer.

M.T. Just you?

Lewis Yes. But again, through the casting advisor.

M.T. Right.

Lewis Individual directors cast individual parts for their particular show. But there aren't all that many you see. These days we tend to have quite a lot of semi-regulars who are in for a few weeks or a couple of months, or three months, or whatever. And that's done always through the casting advisor.

M.T. Is there any chance for an actor, who comes in to play a small part, having their character built up to be a 'regular' part?

Lewis Yes, that happens quite a lot actually . . . You know, you come in and make a reasonable mark – and the character's a useful one – and it gets picked up. That happened particularly to an actor I remember. He came in to play a character just for an odd episode. Then people liked what he did, and the writer wrote him in again, and he came in for another episode . . . then, you know, he came in for a spell . . . and so it builds up.

M.T. What other qualities do you think, apart from ability, are important for an actor to possess?

Lewis The main thing is speed of work. The trouble is there isn't any time for the niceties of normal production. You er . . . (a slightly embarrassed chuckle) I mean even our interviews seem to take a shorter time than anyone elses. You're in and you're out . . . you've either made your mark or you haven't! But they're a very welcoming cast, and people generally are made very welcome. It's a nice place to work . . . but it happens so quickly . . . I mean when I was directing here on one occasion, I'd actually directed an actor from up in a window before I'd even *met* him. (He laughs.) And I mean it *does* happen. And I think that does throw some actors because there's no easing yourself into it. So you've got to have a lot of confidence. You've really got to be sure of yourself. And then I think you'll find you'll fit in very happily.

M.T. So time-keeping is obviously very important.

Lewis It's absolutely vital for us, because we can't afford . . . you know, we're looking at shooting a scene in ten minutes . . . one can put an hour on at the end of the day and . . . we can't afford to. All our regulars know that. In some ways it's more important to be on time, (laughs) than to be good, unfortunately.

M.T. What other qualities are you looking for, given the talent?

Lewis Talent, obviously, is the most important . . . people need to come with their own conception of what the part is, and be confident. They can't expect to get a lot of help. Nobody has the time to give them a lot of help. And knowing the lines. I mean knowing the lines as written on the page and not paraphrasing them.

M.T. How often are the lines changed just before shooting?

Lewis Not a tremendous amount.

M.T. So they haven't got to be able to take a lot of changes on the day?

Lewis No. No, we wouldn't normally expect them to . . . though there are sometimes the exceptional cases when something has happened . . . but no. (Pause) Actually I think the interview is a very important moment for the actor because sometimes an actor in a small part will learn more about the part at the interview than he will when he comes to do it, because there's marginally more time. I mean you do hear yourself at auditions explaining the part in some detail. And you think, you know, if the actor – one of those actors who normally gets the part – actually *listens*, then that's really the sort of rehearsal period very often. (He chuckles)

M.T. Then you just (laughs) . . . do it. Fast!

Lewis Yes, do it! You know I actually feel very sorry for young actors who come into a show like this, because there just isn't that *time*. In the old days you'd come in to a read through and you'd be able to just ease yourself into it, whereas now, you're just THERE!

In spite of what Leonard said about the speed of the schedule, there is, in fact, time for a director to be helpful to the actors, and not just in a technical way either.

Personally, I've developed a shorthand for giving notes 'on the run' – a sort of telegramese: *not so much in 'C' Major* = forget where the camera is and direct the scene towards your partner; *A bit OTT* = you're over-acting; *A bit more* = you're *under*-acting; *Relax on it* = you're nervous and it shows; *Don't anticipate* = you're not listening to what your partner's saying, otherwise you wouldn't say your lines the way you do; *A bit more variety* = you're pretty boring; etc.

A sensitive actor will be aware of the underlying meaning of these notes and take appropriate action. Not many directors enjoy being unkind. Try to interpret truncated notes for yourself, without having to have them spelled out. And whatever you do, don't get involved in long debating arguments with your director, especially if you can see his mind is racing with other matters, and in this sort of set up it usually will be.

Coronation Street is undoubtedly the UK's most popular soap, and it's worth looking at it in some depth. I often feel that actors are ignorant of what is going on around them, and that if they were better informed it would enable them to have much more awareness, and consequent involvement, with the shows they are concerned with. I suppose that's why I hate digital watches – they narrow and concentrate my thoughts on the present, whereas a clock with a face enables me to appreciate the past and the future as well. A more balanced view.

Coronation Street was first transmitted on Friday, December 9th, 1960, in the north of England, by Granada Television; the transmission pattern in those early days was Friday (which was live) and Monday, which was tele-recorded (a system whereby the television picture was filmed, before videotape was invented). When the programme was taken by the Network (transmitted throughout the country by all the other stations), the pattern was changed to Monday/Wednesday. In October 1989 a third episode was added and transmitted on Friday. It's incredible that, all these years later, *Coronation Street* is still the country's most popular television show and consistently tops the ratings.

On average there are about fourteen writers working for the programme at any one time, together with three storyline writers and a programme historian.

There are always at least three stories running through any one episode, and they try to maintain a balanced mix of comedy and drama. Of course there are exceptions – if they are involved in a dramatic funeral episode for instance, they won't bang in a knockabout comedy scene just for the hell of it.

The production schedule is geared to a four-week turn-round, of three episodes recorded a week; so that there are always

A tracking shot being set up on *Coronation Street*. Note the wedges under the tracks to keep them level and two elderly extras (far left) waiting to be given an 'action' cue

four directors involved at any one time; two in preparation, one 'at it', and the other editing and dubbing the previous week's recordings.

A significant chunk of the director's preparation period will be spent studying the rehearsal scripts and from them making out a camera script. This is a detailed camera interpretation of the action as he sees it, which will only be distributed to the technicians. Actors always work from the rehearsal script, and will only see a camera script, usually by chance, in the studio. But just to help dispel some of the mystique that can get in the way of an actor's comprehension of the television process, I've included a sample in the next chapter, see page 81. It's over simplified but the more technically curious of you will get the gist, while the rest of you can ignore it.

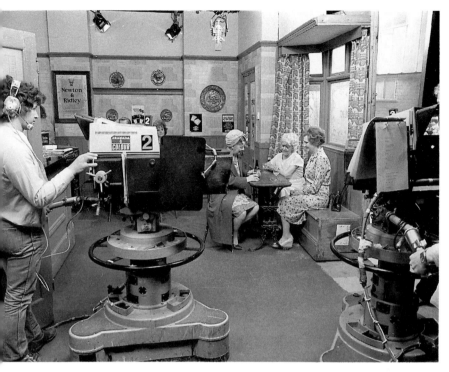

A quiet studio scene in the old Rover's Return c. 1982. Note the left hand door has been taken off its hinges and most of the furniture removed to make space for the cameras

The six day production week starts off with exterior shooting on the Sunday and Monday, while Tuesday and Wednesday are rehearsal days for the studio recording of Thursday and Friday. If you're a 'regular', Saturday is probably your only day off. It sounds like hard graft, and it is, but you can negotiate generous time off (episodes out) with the producer if you are sufficiently organised in advance.

During rehearsals you will have a chance to talk to the wardrobe and make-up departments about your studio requirements.

On Wednesday afternoon there is what is known as a 'technical run', which takes place in the rehearsal room. Some of the technical crew assigned to your studio will be there, so that any problems that might arise can be anticipated. The producer will also be there, just to make sure things are on course, and perhaps the writer if they're available. *Coronation Street* is particularly well-organised and, in my opinion, incorporating 'technical' and 'producer's' run-throughs (not usual on most soaps) saves valuable time.

The 'tech run' also gives the PA a chance to get a final estimate of the overall running length of each episode (ideally 24 minutes 35 seconds). An over-long episode is not usually a problem as it can easily be cut; not so if an episode is running short in which case last minute 'spreads' may have to be written – and you'll have to learn them! I should add that changes are rarely called for as the serial is so well-written.

The Thursday and Friday recording days are from 9.00 am to 6 pm. Each scene is rehearsed until everyone is happy and it's then 'banged in the can' (recorded). The scenes are more often than not recorded out of sequence, usually in 'set order' (do all the scenes set in the pub before moving on to the shop, etc.) It saves time if you move the 'ironmongery' (cameras, etc.) about as little as possible.

The 'rehearse/record' syndrome has its problems for the actor. Not least of which are either anticipating or remembering the state of mind and/or pace you played scenes that will eventually be interspersed with the one you are currently involved in. That's why sticking to 'story order' rehearsals for as long as possible is a help, because it gives you time to mark things out mentally.

The director and his PA move into the editing suite early the following week and on the Monday, if the director is 'on a roll', he will have collected his next three scripts. No rest for the wicked!

The finished programmes are transmitted three weeks later, on Monday, Wednesday and Friday.

Although 'soaps' can offer an actor unhoped for financial security, the old question of 'Should I, or shouldn't I take the job?' can only be answered individually. Personally I would think that most good actors can easily survive a year, maybe two, without their future being compromised by acting in a serial. It depends on several factors: an actor who is already well-established in the profession and has therefore made a lot of contacts is much more likely to find work quickly when they leave the cast than someone who's only claim to fame is being in that show. Versatility, age and attitude are all to be taken into account, as well as a willingness to plough pastures new. Certainly the least likely actors to succeed in a post-soap career are those who sit around fooling themselves that they have 'made it'. The phone might never ring again.

What a business eh? You're a household name (at least your character is) one minute, but as soon as you leave, either you're too well-known as that character to get a job playing others, or, as can happen, the director you'd hoped to meet won't see you because he's never watched your particular 'soap' and has never even heard of you!

Many actors find solace (and money) in touring stage plays that capitalise on their 'soap' image. There are several theatrical managements who specialise in this sort of exploitative casting. The danger is that the actor is only putting off the day of reckoning, and might be better advised to shed the image altogether as soon as possible. That said, it's a hard decision, particularly once you've got used to all that lovely, regular loot!

Chapter Seven
Rehearsing and Recording

When you first arrive at the rehearsal room, particularly if you have a small part in a long-running, well-established programme, you'll probably be very nervous. Don't be. Almost without exception, the regular actors (if you're working on a series or serial) will go out of their way to be friendly and say 'hello'. Of course, there will be an established camaraderie amongst the regulars, so don't try to push your way into circles until you are invited to, or compensate for your insecurity by telling everyone what a big shot you are. Actors in regular employment are singularly unimpressed by this sort of talk! Make sure that the opulent chair you've decided to sit in isn't tacitly reserved for the star of the show, and observe quietly rather than diving in head first.

If it's your first experience of a television programme, you may be non-plussed to find the floor marked up in different coloured tape. These colours will represent rooms and acting areas which relate to the set in the studio (a different colour for each) and you'll probably find that doorways are represented by poles stuck in hollow metal sleeves. Take time to acquaint yourself with the layout of any 'sets' that involve you, and if in doubt, ask the ASM (Assistant Stage Manager) or FM (Floor Manager) to explain the layout to you. These floor markings can be very confusing unless carefully explained. Sometimes there may be a model of the set for you to look at, but they are usually only on display if you're doing a 'one off' play, and long-running shows will have discarded theirs after the first few episodes have been recorded.

Make sure you always arrive ten or fifteen minutes before you are 'called'. The ASM will always let you know what time you are supposed to be at rehearsals, and very often you'll be given a schedule listing the calls for the week. As the recording

dates approach, you'll also be given a schedule for the studio as well.

If you have the luxury of rehearsing, in my opinion it's best to start off with a muted performance (even if you're quite sure what you will be doing eventually) so that you have somewhere to 'go'. So often I've seen beautiful performances being given in the rehearsal room, only to be disappointed by the finished result. Usually, this is because the actor has 'peaked' before the recording. Just like an athlete, you must pace yourself, so that you are at your best when it matters most.

Every director works differently, according to his or her personality. 'One off' dramas, some series and situation comedies normally begin the rehearsal process with a 'read-through' of the script. Everyone sits round a large table, usually with the director and his cohorts, which could include the producer, the writer, the script editor and the PA, grouped together, whilst the cast sit round in no particular order. It can be quite daunting if you are inexperienced. For a start, you aren't quite sure where to sit – that's another good reason to arrive early on the first day, as it gives you time to talk to a few people whose lead you can then follow. Another insecurity arises over what kind of reading to give – a pretty good indication of how you intend to play the part, or an almost inaudible mumble that some actors, particularly well-known ones, tend to give. I advise a middle course; don't show off your grasp of the character, but do imbue the reading with a little life. Don't forget that everyone else will be nervous, but 'read-throughs' are always punctuated with nervous laughs and there's a big sigh of relief when they're over. Personally, I think they are of limited value, but they do give the PA a chance to get an idea of the running time, the writer his first chance to see if it reads reasonably well, and for the cast, it is at least an ice-breaker.

Jot down the names of the other actors if you're formally introduced, so that you can avoid having to ask their name when you next talk to them. We are all flattered and impressed if someone has noted our names on a fleeting introduction, and tend to remember theirs as a result.

There often isn't a script read-through these days, so don't be surprised if this nicety is dispensed with.

If you are involved in an episode of a soap, you will find yourself 'blocking it' before you do anything else. This involves quickly going through the moves the director has worked out. You will be told where to move to, when to turn, and when to sit, etc. Make sure you arrive at rehearsals equipped with a well-sharpened pencil, because you will need one here – don't think you will remember your moves, because you won't. Write them down when they are given to you. Subsequently, if you are in any doubt, you can check with the stage manager, who jots down all the moves.

'Blocking' the piece will be very fast, and don't waste time arguing. Just do as you are asked. You may feel that your moves could be improved, but there's rarely time to alter what the director has (hopefully) painstakingly worked out, so try to make them work.

The reason the director will give you such specific moves (much more so than in the theatre), is that he has carefully worked out each move, bearing in mind the shots he wants to take. A camera script, incorporating your given moves will usually have been prepared *before* you even rehearse, so if there are subsequent changes, it can involve a good deal of re-jigging from the technical point of view.

During the next few days of rehearsal you will use 'standby' props and furniture, (unless you're actually rehearsing on the set), which will be approximate to the ones you will find in the studio. If you have a complicated bit of business to do, involving a prop, and you are being 'thrown' by not having the actual article, ask the stage manager if it's possible for you to have the real thing the next time you do the scene. It often is. Food can also be a problem, so make sure, if you're supposed to eat a meal during the course of a scene, that you are given something that's easy to eat. Avoid scrambled eggs at all costs; it tends to stick to your teeth and makes very unpleasant viewing! Never push food around on your plate – it only draws attention to the fact that you're not eating it.

Make sure that you are given something that's easy to eat

Because the furniture is only an approximation of the real thing, don't get thrown when you find it's *totally* different when you get into the studio. In fact, it's essential to have a good look around the studio, on your own if you can, just to try things out before you are officially called.

You'll find during rehearsals, that the director and his assistants will tend to invade your space, i.e. stand uncomfortably close to you when playing a scene. Don't let this put you off. In the studios, you'll have all the ironmongery to cope with, so look upon it as a good practice! You'll also find directors have a nasty habit of just turning on their heels at the end of your emotional scene with never a word (except perhaps a click of the fingers) and going over to where the next scene is taking place. If he says 'good', 'well done', or simply 'fine', count yourself lucky, but don't get upset if you aren't praised – it's simply a question of time.

Learn your lines as quickly as possible, so that you are free to concentrate on the performance.

Usually the day before you go into the studio, you will have two rather tiresome 'run-throughs'. One will be for the producer, who will want to see what everyone is up to. He or she will usually be accompanied by the script editor, who wants to check that the script is working. This run will often be done in 'story order', i.e. as the script was written. Actors tend to get rather scared at this point, for it's the nearest thing they get to performing for an audience. It can be a tremendous let-down, for a lot of producers have no idea how actors tick, and rarely give words of praise or encouragement. All too often, they are more concerned that the performers are sticking to the script, and, eyes firmly down, they miss the nice touches and subtleties brought to it by the actors. Sometimes, however, you'll be lucky, and get a word of praise – cherish it and press it into your diary, you won't get many.

The 'technical run-through' is for the benefit of the technicians and will always be done in 'recording order', i.e. the order in which the scenes will be recorded (except on *Coronation Street*, where, as I explained in the previous chapter, it is incorporated into the producer's run).

Before your recording day/s begin, check that you have taken steps to know the answers to the following questions:

1. What time are you called for make-up? (No you don't do your own, but if you have sensitive skin or think you look best in a certain shade of lipstick, talk this over with the make-up supervisor BEFORE the studio date.)

2. Will my costume be in my dressing-room waiting for me, or do I have to get it from the wardrobe department myself? (Usually the former, unless you've been asked to bring something of your own in to wear, but CHECK FIRST.)

3. Do I need to be in costume for the first rehearsals on camera? (Usually, but often not if you're performing in a situation

comedy, which doesn't work on the 'rehearse record' principle – see page 129.)

4. Do I collect my dressing-room key from reception or security, or will it be open? And how do I find my dressing-room anyway? (Either. Very often, if you have an early call, before main reception is open, it will be left with the car park security people. Try to find out how you get to the dressing-room area before the day if possible. You want to minimise the stress of coping with the unfamiliar.)

5. What do I do with my costume and key at the end of the day? (Usually leave the former neatly folded on a hanger in your dressing-room, and hand the latter in to reception. Once again, check in advance.)

6. Can I take crockery from the canteen into my dressing-room so I can have a quiet meal break on my own? (Depends on the studio policy. If yes, make sure you return all the items when you leave, or the studio might quickly change this policy!)

7. Where can I watch scenes, that I'm not in, being recorded? (Usually in make-up or wardrobe, but don't get in the way. Sometimes there is a viewing room for this purpose. Certainly, don't hang about on the studio floor when you're not needed.)

8. Can I smoke in the studio? (No, unless you have to during the course of a scene.)

9. Can I invite my mum and dad to the studio to show them around in the lunch hour? (No, unless you've asked and been given permission by the floor manager/producer/security, etc. It's not easy to get people in to the studio complex, but if you really want to meet someone in the building, make sure you ask well in advance of the day.)

10. Is it alright to have a drink in the club bar at lunchtime? (Most studios have 'members only' clubs, so you may need to get someone to sign you in. If you do, it's a good idea to resist the temptation of alcohol until after the recording.)

11. Can I just wander off anywhere I like when I've done my scene, so long as I'm back in time for my next one? (No. schedules change frequently. Always let the ASM or studio assistant – someone designated to find and fetch artists on the day – know *exactly* where you'll be.)

12. Is it safe for me to make social arrangements around the studio schedule? (No. Once more, schedules change. Don't make any important social arrangements when you're involved in a studio recording.)

If you are involved in the first scene to be recorded, you may well find upon entering that the cameras are all standing next to each other pointing at a 'test card'. This means that they are in 'line up' – the pictures that they are sending are being adjusted by the TOM (Technical Operations Manager) to make sure they are registering the same compatible information. Don't cross between them and the card, or you'll get in the way. In fact, you'll spend most of your day keeping 'out of the way', as you will learn – even sometimes when you're on set!

You might come across a camera script once you're in the studio, and for the benefit of those of you who are interested, I'll try to give you a short guide to interpreting them. However, I don't recommend that you spend hours going through one just to see how many close-ups you've got, for this can lead to para-noia! Most good actors just get on with playing the part – though it can be handy to know if the camera is going to be close on you or not in some situations. If in doubt, ask your director – he'll tell you, I'm sure.

Here's a sample of the camera script of a short pub scene. At the top left of the first page you will see that there are three cameras to be used in the scene: camera 1 is in position 'A', 2 in position 'C', 3 in position 'F'. At the top right you will see that there is only one sound boom, and it is in position 'A'. These positions will be marked up on the studio floor plan, copies of which the technicians keep by them. Visual require-ments are always indicated to the left of the script and the sound requirements to the right. 'FX' means sound effects. The shots are numbered in order, followed by the number of the camera which is to take the shot, with a brief, always abbrevi-ated, description – frgnd (foreground), a/b (as before), etc. The tick at the end of a line: / indicates the point where the 'cut' takes place; if an 'open' line is scripted: _____ it means that the shot will be cut according to the action and not the words. All the scripted shots will also be listed on individual 'camera cards' which are clipped to the sides of the cameras as a quick reference for the operators.

Directors vary their terminology, but the following is a guide to the size of shots that have been scripted; they are followed by a description of the subject: *W/A* = wide angle, usually encompassing the entire action; *M/S* = mid-shot, waist high; *3S* = include 3 people; *C/2S* = close as you can get to the following 2 people; *L/S* = long shot, full length; *MCU* = medium close up, chest height; *CU* = close up, full head; *BCU* = big close up, cut off the hair. You'll also find descriptions to help the cameraman, like; *Pan* = follow the person/thing as it moves, with the lens; *Crab L* or *R* = (move the actual camera left or right); *Pull back* = physically pull the camera away from the subject; *Push in* = the reverse; *Tighten* = zoom in; *Open out* = the reverse.

The difference between a 'tighten' and a 'push' is important to note. If the zoom is used, the background gets flattened, whereas a 'push' maintains the same ratio of space between the subject and their background and therefore retains an element of 3D.

Try following the script – yes I know you're not technicians, but I honestly feel it's good for actors to increase their knowledge of the medium in which they work.

The technique used in studios is almost invariably 'rehearse and record'. That means that you will rehearse a scene, and once the director and crew are happy with the way it looks, sounds, and is being played, it will be recorded. One of the disadvantages to this method of recording, from the actors' point of view, is that if you only appear in a couple of scenes, and they are recorded early in the day, you can be left 'up in the air' once you've finished. It often happens that the rest of the cast continue recording, and the director hasn't got time to say goodbye to you personally. You feel insecure about how good or bad you were, and to crown it all, the pubs aren't even open yet! In the theatre, you all (usually) finish the performance, then can wind down together. Being a social animal, the 'rehearse and record' technique can be most unsatisfying, but, like anything else, forewarned is forearmed, and you'll get used to it.

Cameras 1A/2C/3F

Boom Pos. A

INTERIOR: COACH & HORSES, DAY

FX
JUKE BOX

1 1 W/A Man big frgrnd

A FEW PEOPLE SEATED AT SCATTERED TABLES.
MIDDLE AGED MAN IS DRINKING AT THE BAR.
MAUREEN & DEIDRE COME IN AND LOOK ROUND. THEY
SEE TERRY & JIM HAVE NOT ARRIVED & STAND
UNCERTAINLY AT THE BAR.

MAUREEN: (looks at watch) Well sod this for a
lark. They're not here either. D'you think the
buggers have stood us up?

DEIDRE: Sods if they 'ave. We might as well
hang on here for a bit, there's nowhere else
to go at this time of night. Let's 'ave a
drink anyway.

2 3 M/S Deidre
pan her to 2S
with Barman

as she rises.

SHE TRIES TO CATCH THE EYE OF THE YOUNG BARMAN
WHO IS WASHING THE GLASSES AT THE FAR END OF
THE BAR, BUT INSTEAD CATCHES THE EYE OF THE

3 2 3S Man/Deidre
Maureen

MIDDLE-AGED MAN, WHO SMILES INGRATIATINGLY AND
WAVES HIS GLASS AT THEM.

MAN: Can I buy you charming ladies a drink?

DIEDRE: (Under her breath) Oh bugger off.
(Aloud) Ta very much but we're waiting for
people.

MAN: (Weaving unsteadily towards them) No
reason not to wet your whistles in advance.
I'm waiting for my wife, but she's not stopped
me partaking while waiting, if you'll pardon

4 1 C/2S Maureen/Deidre

the expression.

MAUREEN: (Sotto voice) I'll say. (She looks at
Deidre) Oh what the hell! We're broke anyway.
Thanks ever so. I'll have a sha...campari and
orange please.

5 2 a/b

DEIDRE: Yeah, me too, ta.

MAN: (To barman) Two campari and orange, and
another double for me, Digger. (To girls) I
must say, I think your young men must need
their heads seeing to, leaving you two here at

6 3 M/S barman

a loose end. (To barman) Don't you agree
Crocodile?

7 1 a/b
pan Maureen to bar
include door

BARMAN: Yeah, too right.

8 2 a/b pull back to
4S as boys enter

THE GIRLS GIGGLE. FLATTERED IN SPITE OF
THEMSELVES. MAUREEN DRAPES HER CLEAVAGE ON THE
BAR. DEIDRE THROWS BACK HER HEAD AND CATCHES
THE BARMEN'S EYE. TERRY & JIM ENTER. THEY ARE
DISHEVELLED AND IN A FOUL MOOD. THEY 'SUS' THE
SCENE IMMEDIATELY.

JIM: Well you bleedin' slags - couldn't you
have waited for us without chattin' up the
whole place. (To barman) Couldn't you take
your eyes off her tits you Ozzie letch?

TERRY: And you can stick your eyes back in you
drunken old bugger.

9 3 CU barman	MAN: Now look here...
10 1 4S a/b	BARMAN: Don't you speak to me like that you Pommie ponce...
	MAUREEN: We were only having a drink for God's sake. What's the matter with you two?
11 2 CU Arm on bar open out to 2S Man/Maureen	DEIDRE: So where the hell have you been anyway?...
	JIM REACHES TO GRAB MAUREEN'S ARM. AS HE DOES SO HE KNOCKS THE MAN'S ARM OFF THE BAR, WHO STAGGERS AND THROWS HIS DRINK ALL OVER DEIDRE.
12 1 L/S Door woman enters pan her to group	DEIDRE: Oh no! Look what you've done, you silly old bugger.
	THE MAN LURCHES FORWARD INTO MAUREEN. AT THIS MOMENT A MIDDLE AGED WOMAN MARCHES IN. SHE IS HORRIFIED AT THE SCENE WHICH CONFRONTS HER.
	WOMAN: Fred! leave that girl alone. (Seizing Maureen) Leave him alone you little tart.
	DEIDRE: (Seizing her) Get off mi mate - it's your rotten husband's fault.
13 MCU Deidre	TERRY: Your fault you mean. Oggling the two of them. I saw yer.
14 4S Terry/Deidre/ Maureen/Jim	DEIDRE: (Shoving him) I don't know what you mean... coming in here and accusing us like that! Where've you been all night anyway?
	TERRY: Don't you shove me!
	MAUREEN: I'm fed up with all this, I'm going home.
15 2 MCU woman	DEIDRE: Me too - look at me blouse...ruined (to WOMAN) You should 'ave him locked up!
16 3 MCU man Develop to 2S Jim/Barman	WOMAN: (Ignoring her) Come on Fred, let's be off.
	MAN: (Feebly) I'll just have another little double.
	WOMAN: Certainly not. Let's get you home while you're still on your feet.
	THEY EXIT UNSTEADILY FX POLICE SIREN
17 1 CU Maureen	JIM: You two can't piss off now - we've only just got here.
18 2 2S Maureen/ Barman	MAUREEN: Well that's not our fault is it? Come on Dee. (To Barman, seductively) Sorry about your nice clean bar.
19 3 L/S Girls	BARMAN: No sweat. Drop in again anytime...
20 1 2S Boys pan them to door	MAUREEN AND DEIDRE, ARM IN ARM, MINCE OUT. THE BOYS FOLLOW, ARGUING AMONG THEMSELVES. THE BARMAN SMILES TO HIMSELF AND WIPES THE COUNTER.
21 1 M/S Barman push in to MCU as he wipes bar	END OF SCENE TAPE STOP

Some directors will finely rehearse before they record. (Personally, after a couple of run-throughs, I like to 'rehearse on tape' – just *in case* everybody gets it right.) Over the years, I've found that more often than not, a cast and crew are just that bit sharper when it comes to the first attempt at recording; their adrenalin is pumping round and there is the added spontaneity that goes with a first attempt at anything. It doesn't always work, of course, and you can end up having half a dozen takes before a scene is finally 'in the can'.

Any scene involving pubs, shops, and cafes, that has a lot of people eating or drinking in it always seems to take forever to get right – so be patient.

Some directors like to work 'on the floor', which means literally that, so as to keep personal contact with the actors and crew for as long as possible. They will always 'go upstairs' back to the control room to monitor a 'take', but I think actors like this approach, as it's always easier to talk face to face with your director rather than relay conversations through the floor manager. You'll notice that the FM has headphones and a transmitter, so that they can do just that. He or she is the person who takes sole charge of the proceedings in the studio, and even the director, as a matter of courtesy, asks the FM if they mind him working on the floor.

When you rehearse a scene don't forget to keep a little of your energy in reserve for the actual 'take', or you might end up exhausted. This is one example of where the techniques you have acquired can be put into practice.

Be aware of what you say in the studio. Booms are often left 'open', and it might not go down too well with your director if you are heard to say things like, 'What the hell's he doing, farting around up there'. There are many technicalities to attend to, and you will rarely be aware of everything that is going on.

If you are involved in any scenes with a telephone, make sure you know exactly what's going to happen on the day. Sometimes in a two-handed conversation, the director may want to 'hold' on you while the person at the other end speaks. He may, or may not want the audience to hear what the other person is saying. If he doesn't, fine, all you have to do is to act the pauses. But sometimes (and I must admit this is rare these days as most additional sounds are mixed in at the edit), you

A 'Vinten Heron' camera at Alexandra Palace in 1949, Videotape hadn't been invented, so actors had to perform 'live'

may have a real two-handed conversation. Whatever – check on it at rehearsals.

Telephone conversations always feature heavily in 'soaps' – it's the quickest way to get reported events to the characters – it's also the laziest. Years ago, the long running serial, *Crossroads*, was timed to the exact second. It was recorded 'as live', and each episode lasted nineteen minutes and thirty seconds. There were no editing facilities in the early days and the episode was recorded in two solid chunks; part one, from the opening titles to the commercial break, and part two, which also embraced the closing captions. Sometimes, during the recording, scenes 'spread' and took longer than anticipated. For those of you who remember the saga, this accounted for the whizzing by of the end credits as the director struggled to bring the show in on time. If scenes tightened up, however, it was common practice to ask Noelle Gordon, the star of the show, to make a phone call at the end of one of her endless sitting room scenes and 'order some groceries'. A message would be got to her via the floor manager during a scene in which she was not involved, and lo and behold, at the end of her scene 'Nollie' would pick up the phone and do the necessary. She was so good at these ad-libs that she could be 'counted down' to the second, by the F.M. standing close by her, ticking off his fingers. After she had replaced the receiver she would look soulfully left of camera and sigh – that was the cue for the director to 'cue and cut' to the next scene. Ah yes . . . I remember it well!

Sometimes, you might find yourself on a sofa, all ready to play a love scene, when the FM will ask you to get up while the sofa is jacked up on wooden blocks. These small stepped blocks are called 'two, four, sixes', because each step is, respectively, two, four, and six inches high. The cameras have a minimum height from which they can operate, and if the furniture is particularly low, it might need raising. This can be quite disconcerting if you're a short actor, to suddenly find your legs dangling in the air as you propose marriage in a romantic setting! You may be also asked to walk or sit down at a slower pace than you've rehearsed. This is because your moves have to be contained by the camera and, especially if they are on a 'tight' lens, they may experience difficulty.

You may be asked to vacate the set for a number of reasons, often while lamps are adjusted and carpets rolled back, but it's all part and parcel of the game, so don't let it throw you.

You have to master many distractions in the studio; make-up and wardrobe people will constantly be popping on to the set to freshen you up or adjust your collar, props will disappear only to be replaced by other items, and sometimes whole scenes will be totally re-jigged from beginning to end, or cuts suddenly made. You'll also have to get used to extra actors suddenly appearing, particularly in pub scenes, to make the place 'peopled', and it can be quite disturbing suddenly to find there are half a dozen people to wade through on your way to the bar. Try not to think of extra artists as some sort of inferior acting species – many famous actors have emerged from their ranks, so try and make them feel as comfortable and at ease with you as possible. They have a particularly difficult role to play, being totally unfamiliar with what is expected of them until they arrive.

Usually, 'extras' are directed through the floor manager, and their background reactions can often make or break a scene. If you are offered work as an extra, or seek it through an agency specialising in this field, you might think it worthwhile to accept. At least you will get the feel of a studio while being under no pressure to perform a difficult role. In my day, as a young actor, I 'walked on' in several productions, and found the experience invaluable.

Try to keep your chatter down to a minimum (I know it's often nerves) whilst on the set. As I said, booms are often 'open', and excessive noise on the floor can be very distracting for people who are trying to think and make important decisions. Floor managers, whose job it is to ensure the smoothness of the operation have better things to do than continually shout 'Keep the noise down PLEASE!', yet it seems the most common cry of all. You can help. And don't think behaviour and demeanour on the set won't be noticed – it certainly will. Working with a young, often inexperienced actor can be very rewarding, particularly if they conduct themselves well. Producers and directors take note of such things and remember them when they are next casting. It's not just how good you are that matters, it's how nice you are to work with that's important too.

You'll notice that when a camera is 'on air', it shows a red light, and in a multi-camera situation, where whole scenes are shot in one 'take', you will sometimes be in shot and sometimes not, but don't ever drop out of character – it will ruin your concentration. Try to ignore the camera and other movements on the set, and simply put into practice all that you've rehearsed. Often re-takes will be necessary. These can occur at any time, either during a scene or after the completion of a 'take'. Try to recapture the exact mood and pace of the previous one, because when the show is finally edited, the director may want to intercut between two versions, and this can only be done if one matches the other .

Often, scenes will be played back so that you can view them on the monitors on the floor. Some actors are thrown by watching themselves in this way, so if you feel easier going off into a corner whilst this is going on, do so – nobody will think it odd behaviour. Do not, however, ask if you can see a playback, unless you have a very good reason, because there may not be time.

I hope at the end of your first studio day, when the floor manager says 'Thanks folks, that's a wrap', you've had a thoroughly satisfying time.

Chapter Eight
Corporates and Commercials

Probably the best thing to happen to actors since the invention of the moving image was the application of that development to business affairs. I can't think of a single actor, who has been in the business for more than five minutes, who has not had his rent paid by an appearance in either a corporate communication or a commercial; probably several. The wonderful thing about them is that they usually turn up unexpectedly. Just when you thought you had better stop calling yourself an actor because it's been so long since you worked, you get a job which will keep you going for another couple of weeks, or months – even, in the case of a long running television advertising campaign, years.

Corporate Communications used to be called industrial films, are sometimes called business communications, and are more often than not shot on video. Whatever their initial format (the word used to describe the storage method of an image – 35 or 16 mm film, 1 inch or Betacam SP tape, all of which are acceptable to broadcasters) they usually finish up on VHS (the format used by domestic video recorders). This is because VHS machines are readily available in most situations and a reasonable quality can be preserved if the initial recorded image has been made using a broadcast format. U-Matic tape, which is a sort of half-way format, will give better reproduction than VHS but is not so good to initiate on. If you ever make a showreel of your work, ask the company if you could buy (or borrow) a U-Matic copy of the programme, rather than VHS, as the quality will be that much better when you make copies.

Corporate videos serve a wide variety of purposes: staff training; point of sale (the sort of things you see while queuing in the Post Office); public relations (this is how good we are);

video records (construction companies often chart the progress of various works); medical information (to update GP's on product availability and new techniques); video brochures (holiday companies and estate agents); 'How to Do It' video manuals (mend the car, boil an egg, etc.). In fact the application for business video is limitless.

Although production of these videos has diminished in recent years, due to the recession, their variety and scope has increased, so there is still a reasonable amount of work about.

A large proportion of these programmes are made by small, independent companies, some one-man bands, and a number by highly specialised groups, particularly in the medical field. Practices vary wildly, but as far as you are concerned, casting tends to be a little more relaxed than their commercial counterparts. Because of the difference in budgets (it always seems to come down to loot in the end!), corporates are the poor relations, and while a large company like, say, B&Q, will employ an agency to take charge of their television advertising, its training managers will liaise directly with a production company. Because the client and the producer work so closely together throughout the whole process it usually results in a happier working environment for the actor. Not, I hasten to add, always!

In America, where the whole entertainment industry is unionised, you would work to the appropriate SAG contract for a 'corporate' job; but in England, in spite of various attempts to organise this muddled section of the business and produce formal agreements, in truth everybody goes about doing their own thing. Some agents insist that a production company signs a contract if they want to use one of their artists, some production companies do the reverse. In my own case (I've produced dozens of these programmes over the years), and in common with most practitioners, I simply write a letter to the artist's agent confirming the dates and money we've discussed over the phone. I've always found this to be perfectly satisfactory, and never once had a dispute. Most agents are very smart about who and who not to trust.

These days you can expect to earn between £250 – £350 a day – possibly a little less if it's a tiny part that only needs a nod and a couple of hours work. This would normally be for a ten hour day, with lunch provided. Additional travel or location expenses would be agreed, if relevant, at the outset, bearing in mind what could be considered to be 'reasonable' by all parties. Overtime, per hour, at a fifth the daily rate is fairly standard. Sometimes you might be asked to negotiate a fee which covers any overtime that may be necessary. This will be because the production company is on a very tight rein and needs to know in advance exactly what its outgoings will be. This is fine, provided it's been agreed before the job takes place. Always sort these things out in advance, then get the arrangements confirmed in writing, so you know exactly where you are.

You may think that acting in corporates is a bit beneath your dignity, especially when you're all bright-eyed and bushy-tailed on leaving drama school. My advice is, take everything you can in the early days (and usually later too), provided you're not being exploited; increase your knowledge and experience.

It's very important, when you go for an interview, that you know what sort of part you are up for. Don't go in jeans and a sweater if you know you're up for the managing director's secretary; obviously a skirt and blouse would be more appropriate. Most companies will have a modest budget for wardrobe, but not always, and from my own experience I can tell you that you can miss a job if it's between you and a guy who has a decent suit! Try to develop a wardrobe that includes items you wouldn't want to wear in real life, but might come in useful for work. In my early days you needed a decent selection of clothes when you appeared in rep but now you need it for corporates.

At the casting session you'll probably find the casting director (if there is one, there often isn't), the producer and or director (often combined) and the client/s. Make sure you know who's who before you go in (ask the receptionist), and try to make a good impression on the client. Remember it's the client who briefs the director, who briefs the casting director, so that's the hierarchy. After the session the team will get together and discuss the people they've seen. They may have taken a few Polaroid shots to remind them of the faces they've seen, or they may have recorded a video, though this is not common for corporates. They'll primarily be concerned with getting the right face to front the *attitude* they want to put across, rather than any great depth, so try to mirror their expectations when you're

being interviewed. Don't take up a lot of time telling them about how you enjoyed understudying Portia at Stratford – it's quite likely half of them won't have heard of *The Merchant of Venice* and the rest will think you're talking about Stratford East! Tell them about how you love to shop in their stores and what wonderful products they sell – it's music to their ears.

Inevitably when someone is absolutely right for a part there will be a unanimous decision, but when it comes to cases that involve clear choices, the client will have the final say. Having said that, I've sometimes persuaded them that, in my humble opinion, their choice is a poser who might *look* right but simply can't act. Sometimes I win.

Unfortunately, through sheer bad manners and rudeness, some companies won't let you know if you haven't got the part, and you can be left high and dry for days or even weeks. Decisions after a casting session are usually swift, and unless there is to be another one, are often made immediately after the session. Give them a couple of days, then get your agent to ring up and check on the outcome if you haven't heard. There's no point agonising. A decent company will let you know anyway.

This malpractice of companies only contacting actors they want, and letting the rest go hang, is pretty rife throughout the business, and doesn't just apply to corporates.

If you get the job you may be contacted by various people, so make sure, if you haven't got a phone, that there is always somewhere for messages to be left. Make-up and wardrobe may want to get hold of you; in any event someone will want to tell you, often at the last minute, what your 'call' is – where and when you are needed, etc. I know it's painfully obvious to always have a pen and paper by you, but I can't tell you the number of hours wasted while someone goes to get something to write with. Do make sure you have your act together, or you can antagonise people before you start.

Try to get a hold of your script as soon as possible. This may not be easy as lines are often rewritten right up to the 'off'. Tell them you'd rather have something than nothing. Then at least you can break the back of it. Don't forget to be prepared for script changes on the day (except for odd words, changes are less likely to occur on commercials).

I remember on one shoot I was directing last year that we were getting script changes by fax from the client's client (yes, even that sometimes happens) at the studio, even as we were shooting. Fortunately the artists involved, Lynda Bellingham and Tim Healey, were very experienced and able to cope but I can't pretend it was easy for any of us.

If you are called upon to 'present' a video, i.e. speak directly to camera, you might be asked to use 'Autocue'. This is a script prompting device which, by the clever use of mirrors, enables

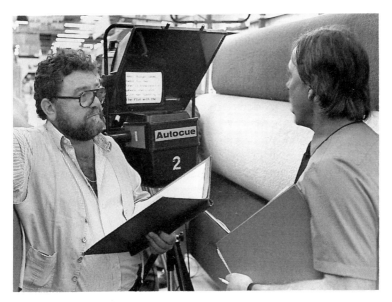

The author, as director, goes through the lines on Autocue with actor Leo Dolin

you to read the text as it appears in front of the camera lens. Using the system needs a little practice – and you need to get the camera at a comfortable distance from you so that the audience can't see your eyes 'scanning' the lines – but most actors can pick the technique up fairly quickly. If you've not used it before, and would feel more confident having a go before the shoot, ask your director if he could contact the company he is using and arrange for you to pop down for a practice when they've got a quiet moment. (Although there is a company called 'Autocue', like 'Hoover', 'Autocue' tends to be a generic term used to cover a lot of slightly different systems). You'll find them immensely helpful people. (Why don't drama schools enlist their help? I'm sure they would charge a minimal rate to introduce their equipment to the uninitiated.)

If you find you are in demand as a presenter, you might get yourself a pair of tailor-made ear-pieces from a hearing centre (about £40). Then get a small dictaphone, which you can tuck away about your person, link it to your earpiece and a remote hand control – and hey-presto you're a portable prompting device! The advantage of this audio prompter, which can be bought as a kit in the United States, is that your movement is not restricted by the distance you need to be from the camera in order to read your lines. Bernard Holley, an actor who first brought it to my attention, tells me 'The trick is to record your lines on to the tape at your intended delivery speed, then say the words three seconds after you hear them. You can 'stop' your remote if there's bits of silent business, then 'play' once more when you start spouting again'. Although it sounds an absolute nightmare to me, I've worked with Bernard when he's used the device, and I can honestly say I've never once seen his eyes water.

A lot of corporate communications are made on location, and though there may be fewer technicians about, the shooting set-up is similar to that for any single camera operation.

In the brief rehearsal time you have (and use every second once you know what the action entails, even while the camera is being set up) make sure you are happy with your position in relation to any props you may have to handle, and that technically at least, you feel confident and happy. A lot of this rehearsal can be done privately, or with someone you're playing a scene with, just to make sure you know the, often difficult and information packed, lines. You may find you have a lot of things to do at once, and it's important to get things straight in your head, so that all your 'business' looks casual and real. Don't, whatever you do, pick up the relaxed attitude of the crew. They are doing these sort of shoots every day, but they're not in front of the camera, they have no lines to put across, no performance to give, and *you* have.

There is a big temptation I know, especially on the first day of a shoot, in a new location, early in the morning, to try to keep relaxed by chatting, sipping coffee, and generally avoiding the coming challenges of the day. It's often borne of insecurity and the feeling that so long as you can put things off and everyone's laughing and joking, somehow the difficulties of doing the job will all magically disappear, and you'll sail through it all. You won't. Any problem you imagined you might have with the part, when you were worrying yourself to sleep the night before, will become reality unless you get your head down as soon as you arrive on location. Let the others lark about, but make sure you're not one of them.

The action taking place off left, is monitored by an engineer (left) and, on a separate screen, by the director, his PA (seated) and the make-up supervisor

If you need to get off into a corner to get yourself together, then this is the time to do it, while things are being moved about and lights set. Always let the production manager, or whoever is in charge of the actors on the day, know where you'll be if needed though, or you'll be cursed (at the very least) if you are suddenly wanted and nobody can find you.

When you actually start shooting, the director, or his assistant, will usually say 'Roll, tape', then there will be a ten second pause, to give the tape time to run up to speed and settle; then you'll hear the engineer say 'Running', or 'Speed'. This is a signal that the director can start the action as soon as he likes, and he will probably say 'Action', or 'Cue', or, in my case sometimes, 'Go'. Whatever, you'll be in no doubt that is the moment for you to do your stuff.

Don't be thrown by retakes. And if you 'dry' it's not the end of the world. Nobody is expecting you to be perfect. The cameraman will probably make a few mistakes too. So don't over-react or get into a panic. Try to keep calm and get on with the job. The biggest difference between a professional and an amateur is not money, it's *attitude*.

There can be any number of technical reasons for retakes, but sometimes they might not be immediately apparent. For instance, everything could seem to be fine, but there may be a sound problem. Only the recordist, who is wearing headphones, might be aware of this because he's the only one listening to the sound as it really is. Unlike film, where the soundtrack is separate and is dubbed later (re-recorded), videotape carries both sound and picture together, and though sound effects are often added, the recorded speech is usually what you get on the finished article. Special attention must therefore be paid to it. Sound quality is often overlooked, yet it can make or break a show. So if the sound engineer says he needs more voice, or asks you to deliver a line a bit more towards the boom (mike), try to oblige. It's in your own interest.

Of course things will go wrong: people will forget things; you'll 'dry'; the camera will break down; it will rain; you'll have a bad lunch, etc. But try not to overreact: keep calm, keep smiling, and, for God's sake, get on with the job! It's a business, not a lark.

The advantage of tape over film, in these circumstances (nothing to do with quality), is that you can replay it instantly to see what you've got 'in the can'. This is particularly useful, not only to make sure the performances and script are right (things can easily be missed during a 'take'), but as a continuity aid. At what speed did you walk off into the next shot? This could be an important reference when you might not do the next shot for days. Polaroid photographs are often used to keep a record for make-up and wardrobe because they can be instantly produced when required. This doesn't mean that you shouldn't concern yourself with continuity. Try to remember which hand you were holding the cigarette in, for example, when you did your big speech; keep an eye on the level of the beer in your glass; was your coat collar turned up or down, for instance, when you entered the room.

Always make a mental note of where the camera is, in relation to your eyeline, when playing a scene. For instance, if the camera is to your right in a wide or 'master' shot, when you come to do your close-ups, you will know that you have to look to the *left* of the lens. If you were to look to the *right* of the lens you would have '*crossed the line*'. Let me explain. Imagine there is an invisible line between you and the person you are addressing. Once the action has been shot from either the left or the right of that imaginary line, the line must never be physically crossed until the action is broken and a new line established. If it *is* crossed it will give the impression that instead of facing the person you are talking to, you will be looking in the same direction as they are.

There are probably more discussions about eyeline positions than anything else, when it comes to doing 'reverses' (close ups, to be cut into a master sequence). The director and cameraman often disagree in their remembrance, so it's definitely 'brownie points' for you if you can be certain!

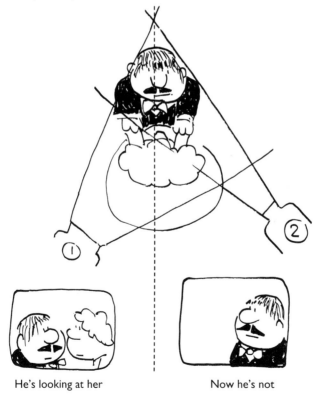

He's looking at her   Now he's not

Cameras must be on the same side of the dotted line

Interactive Video is little understood by many actors, and a good working knowledge of how it operates and how your performance will be used, will help you to focus on the end result. You might even be able to contribute to its making and at the very least, you will know what the discussions are all about during the shoot. I'll try to keep it simple:

Interactive video is mostly used, as far as actors are concerned, for staff training programmes, which have been recorded on tape, then transferred to a video disc. What happens is this; a programme, incorporating all the 'dos and don'ts' of the job, is worked out by the client and a course designer. Let's take the check-out procedure in a supermarket. If a customer wants to pay by credit card, the check-out operator has to make some decisions: for instance, does the store take the card proffered? Is the card valid? Is the card signed, etc. You can pose the various questions to the trainee, and interactive video enables them to see the results of their decisions.

To do this you need a video player (with disc), a computer, a monitor (screen to view) and a keyboard which the trainee uses to activate the computer which in turn activates the video player.

Right, so you're a trainee. You load the disc, and press 'go'. The computer tells the player to start the disc at the beginning and up pops an actor saying, 'Hello, and welcome; this is all about your job . . .' You might then be offered a menu of options and you pick out 'Credit Cards' (you'll always be told which key to press); up comes a scene where somebody offers you a Diners Card and the action 'freezes'. A voice-over and probably a graphic asks you 'Now what do you do?' and gives you three options, 1) Accept the card 2) Accept the card *and* check the signature 3) Tell the customer the store doesn't take Diners Card. You press 1), the computer spools the disc onto that option, and up pops an actor, pretending to be a mate, and tells you that you were wrong because the store doesn't take Diners Card. 'Try again' she says; you press another button and so on. Get the idea? It's 'one to one' training, and as an actor you may be required to record several options. Now that you know this is what happens it may well colour the way you say 'Sorry, that's not right' or 'Quite right, well done' (Tip: never be patronising). As far as the client is concerned, if you are playing the checkout person you'll be his idea of what their checkout staff *should* be like. Inevitably, they won't be, so it's up to you to invest the character with a human face. Try to make employees as real as possible and if the dialogue doesn't sound natural suggest a change. Usually you'll find justifiable changes acceptable, but sometimes the clients have 'bees in their bonnets'! On these occasions it's simply better to 'take the money and run!'

You'll also find that clients tend to include too much information in a script. Not content with covering checkout procedure they also want to bang in a bit about shelf-filling as well. This doesn't usually apply to interactive videos because the programme is specifically designed for a set of questions and answers, but the broader the scope of the video the more likely you are to have to say too much about too many subjects. You won't be able to do anything about it of course, it's a cross you have to bear.

Commercials are very different, and can be more tiresome to make than 'corporates', but the financial rewards are greater (and that's the only reason you'll make them), so be realistic, and put your lips into smile mode as you brace yourself for Take thirty-seven of lifting the little soapy bubbles to your cheek in two and a half seconds.

Time is the essence of commercials. A thirty second commercial may comprise as many as thirty or forty shots. The advertiser must complete the ad within the allotted time, so each shot is carefully timed to ensure that all the action can be accommodated. Story-boards (drawings which illustrate the various shots and dialogue that accompanies them) are carefully constructed, and you will need to complete the requisite action in the given time. Sometimes it's impossible, and the plan is changed, but not often. You can imagine how arduous this can be sometimes, particularly if you have to combine a very difficult line with a tricky piece of action *and* do it all in two and a half seconds. I think that more traditionally well-accomplished actors have broken down in tears of tiredness and frustration in commercial studios than anywhere else!

Commercials are all about gloss and impact (well they have to be, they've only got thirty seconds to convey the whole story). Many commercials aim to grab their audience by identification with the participants, so you will either look right or you won't. You'll be of the right social class or you won't. These are the sort of black and white decisions that have to be made at casting sessions, so to hell with your acting ability; if your face doesn't convey the right message you won't get the part. You will probably go to dozens of sessions and have no luck, but don't let it worry you. Treat each session as a day at the races. If you get the role, your horse has come in. But I can't stress your professional approach too much; remember what Gill Titchmarsh said about actors often being their own worst enemies.

A commercial will probably bring you in £200–£300 for a day's shoot, and repeat screenings nationally could bring thousands more. 'Repeats', as they are called, are based on Television Audience Ratings figures (TVR's). TVR's vary depending on the popularity of the programmes screened, and the population reach, etc. – for instance, you'd get more for one screened in the London ITV region than you would for one screened in East Anglia. This is because the denser the population of a region, the more potential customers the advertiser can reach. These repeat payments are based on a percentage of your daily rate, so the higher your daily rate, the more you will make out of a successful commercial. Although they can be extremely lucrative, they're not as well paid, comparatively, as they were twenty years ago. I remember getting £150 a day, for three days, with repeats based on £150, in 1970, for a series of dog food commercials, and I received over £7,000 within a year. A lot of money in *these* days, let alone *those*. Alan Parker, the director, went on to bigger things, while I slowly returned to earth! The more a commercial is screened, the less your percentage. It's all worked out on a sliding scale that has been agreed with Equity. But don't worry, by the time it's going out at every break you'll have been able to pay the back rent and, hopefully, afford a jolly holiday in the sun.

There is also a thriving 'voice-over' market for commercials, and many well-known personalities, whose voices you may well recognise, prefer to remain visually anonymous, while making a discreet financial killing. Some agents specialise in providing voices solely for this purpose.

Finally – it really is quite depressing how much I seem to be talking about money, but that's the name of the game – if you take on a major commercial series, like Oxo, Maxwell House or Telecom, your agent will probably negotiate a yearly 'buy out' fee. Your contract will stipulate that you can't do any other commercials that may impinge on their particular product range, indeed it's likely you won't be able to make any other commercials at all. You shouldn't worry; your fee will probably be upwards of £50,000 a year. It's not unknown for a television star (better for the manufacturers than a movie star, because as the viewer is used to admitting them into their homes via the telly, they are more likely to buy what they're selling, see?) to be paid £100,000 for a six month 'exploitation' (screening) period.

Taking part in corporates and commercials may well enable you to remain in the business of acting throughout your career, for the discrepancies in fees between 'legitimate' and 'sponsored' work continues to widen as Arts subsidies dwindle.

Chapter Nine
Feature Films

Sadly, at the time of writing, you are less likely to be given a part in a feature film in this country than in any other that considers itself to be a drama producing nation, for we produce the fewest.

Hollywood remains the top of the pile for volume production in the western world, and France has a healthy industry which ironically feeds it – the US moguls have taken to buying up the rights to successful, quality, French films, commissioning a script tailored to their American stars, and launching it as an original on an unsuspecting public. Anyone who first saw and enjoyed *The Return of Martin Guerre*, may have been as surprised as I to see it re-emerge as *Somersby* starring Richard Gere and Jodie Foster. Of course it was the inclusion of those big box-office stars that was the raison d'être for the remake.

We have a strange habit in this country of labelling French films 'arty', whereas in truth most of them, like *Jean de Florette* and *Manon des Sources* are just good commercial films (and are thought of as such in their own country). We're an insular lot there is no doubt – and the Yanks are even worse. Mention 'culture', 'foreign', or 'sub-title' and the majority of film-goers dive for cover. Artificial Eye are the pioneers in marketing foreign, particularly French, films in this country, but their two cinemas in London, the Lumiere and the Renoir, while welcome additions to the facilities of the capital, hardly comprise the sort of distribution network we require if we are to create an atmosphere of universal film appreciation. I wonder if some major brave distributor might put worth ahead of safe commercialism, and encourage their audiences to try something a little different? Fat chance. But I digress.

Italy, Spain, Sweden and Germany all have much healthier industries than our own, but none are as successful as the one in India ('Bollywood' is the popular name for the film centre in Bombay), and they churn out romantic pot-boilers at the rate of knots. Most find their way to this country, and many of the predominantly Asian controlled video duplicating houses founded their empires on the copying of these films, for distribution to the immigrant population. Three times more Indian films are duplicated here than our native counterparts.

Although it was the advent of television, at the beginning of the 1950's that largely destroyed our indigenous film industry, it may well be that, by an ironic twist, it is the television industry that will come to its rescue.

Film on Four, pioneered by David Rose, has long been a flagship for Channel Four, and, like HBO in the States, they continue to invest in the television rights of an ever increasing number of films (*The Crying Game, Howards End, Damage,* etc.). They usually have to wait for two years of cinema exploitation before being able to cash in on their investment and televise the movie.

The BBC's Screens One and Two, on the other hand, have been producing films *specifically* for television, occasionally releasing them for 'theatric' (cinema) release. Films such as *The Snapper, Truly Madly Deeply, Enchanted April,* all made it to the big screen; *post* television. But a new policy has been implemented; until 1996 (at least) the BBC have committed themselves to financing (or co-financing) five feature films a year which will have theatric distribution and video release *before* being transmitted on television. In addition they will also invest in securing the television rights in up to five other independent features. Charles Denton, the BBC's Head of Drama told me 'There may develop a pattern whereby television funded features are released theatrically in foreign countries, but on television in the U.K.'. This is a very exciting development, and though the mooted budgets of 2 million pounds a film is very small beer by modern standards, it's an encouraging start, and by the end of the century you might find you have more opportunities to perform in a feature film than you have at present.

These days it is unlikely that you will experience shooting in a major studio (there aren't many left!), for most films are location orientated. Tracks will be laid, cranes will be hoist, and all manner of ironmongery, rarely seen within the confines of a television back lot, can be daunting to a young actor. Everything seems to be on a larger scale than you are used to – larger crews, more lights, and often a location caterer, who will happily dispense food throughout the day. But these things apart, the acting experience will be identical to shooting any other sort of film. You will probably find, however, that you have a little more time to get yourself together (not a lot) and the atmosphere will be considerably less frenetic than that encountered on a shoot of *The Bill* or *Cheers*, for example.

One of the 'hangovers', if you like, from the leisurely days of film-making that still persists on major features is the employment of 'stand-ins' for the stars, during the lighting process. This arduous business can be very tiring for performers and can save companies a great deal of time and money when setting up a shot.

If you are fortunate enough to work in a studio you will undoubtedly experience a certain frisson at the beginning of a 'take'. Once the director is satisfied that everything is in place and the camera and sound crew are happy with the rehearsal you will often hear the first assistant (a sort of feature film version of the television floor manager) yell 'Red light and bell'. A loud electric bell is then rung to warn everyone to keep quiet because of an impending 'take' and a red light is switched on at all the entrances of the studios to warn people to keep out. At the end of the take the assistant director will yell 'Save the red', an 'all clear' bell will sound and the lights switched off. In common with most actors, I suspect this little ritual is as exciting as anything else you are likely to experience and you'll interpret it as a signal that you aren't just working on trivia; until the film is released that is, when you might suddenly realise, probably for the first time, that you were. What a cynic I've become! Or is it a realist?

I've no experience of directing feature film, but in my younger days I did act in a few. They were all very small parts, but the four experiences I remember best all have a moral, so they're worth recounting.

Tom Jones, The Loneliness of the Long Distance Runner, and *A Taste of Honey* all involved the director Tony Richardson. He was very demanding, enthusiastic (some might say frenetic), and given to eccentricities.

In *Tom Jones* I was asked to play a soldier in the early scenes of Tom's adventures on Dartmoor. This involved a week's work on location in Taunton, and culminated in a short scene where, as a beer-soaked guardsman on night duty, I spotted Tom, whom I presumed had been recently killed in a brawl, running around the outside of an inn. According to the single page of script I'd been sent it looked very straightforward:– THE SOLDIER LOOKS UP, THINKS HE'S SEEN A GHOST, SHOUTS 'THE GHOST WALKS, THE GHOST WALKS', FIRES GUN AND FAINTS.

Tony had an idea which he wanted incorporating into the written action. He decided that when I saw the ghost he'd like my hair to stand on end – literally. After toying with the idea of a trick wig, he'd settled for something much more realistic. 'Malkie darling, I've had a wonderful idea. I've been talking to this guy, who says if you were to stand on a big rubber pad – a thick one mind – and we passed a few thousand volts of electricity through you, your hair would stand on end quite naturally. What do you think honey?'

Although he cackled with laughter at the image he'd created I could see he wasn't joking. Nor was I when I begged him for time to think it over. He gave me two days, which was all he could afford in the busy schedule.

Now it might seem odd to you that I didn't say 'Not on your life' straight away; but remember I was a young and hungry actor, and Tony was a reliable and frequent employer; I didn't want to upset him. So for the next two days a very worried soldier trooped his way through the mists of Dartmoor. I really didn't know what to say to his request. I had visions of being burned to a cinder at a single stroke. What if my rifle touched the ground? Suppose the rubber wasn't thick enough? Perhaps they could try it out on a pig first? Would I ever work again if I said no? Probably not. Notwithstanding years of impending unemployment, I decided that I really couldn't go along with the idea. When the day for my reply dawned, I sought him out and ventured, 'Oh Tony, about that electricity business . . .' 'Oh that', he interrupted, 'I don't think it's a good idea after all, Ray thinks you might get fried'. He paused just long enough to cackle at the thought, 'Sorry babe, it would have been fun, I know.' My sigh of relief must have been louder than Vesuvius erupting. 'What a shame', I murmured inaudibly as I tottered away.

Moral *If you are asked to do something hazardous to your person and feel it beyond the call of your contractual obligations refuse the request at once and without hesitation.*

In *The Loneliness of the Long Distance Runner* I was asked to play a bird impressionist in a prison concert party. When I got to the location, a boys reform school, if my memory serves me right, with the inmates booked as concert party audience, I complained that I hadn't been sent a script. 'But there isn't one sweetie', Tony said, looking surprised. 'Did no-one tell you that you've just got to do your usual show to these nice boys. We want their genuine reaction to your act'. 'But I don't do an act Tony, you know that, let alone bird impressions.' This provoked howls of mirth from Tony who said 'I know honey, but that's the fun of it don't you see. *They* don't know you aren't the genuine *thing*. It will be so much more *fun*. Anyway *everybody* can do bird impressions these days. So *look*, when I introduce you to the boys, just step forward and do your *thing*, we'll find focus if you keep pretty still'. He cackled and left me to it.

I began to sweat, but once I had been 'introduced' to the jeering masses, my legs duly carried me forward to the microphone and I literally ad-libbed a patter and impression act for about ten minutes. It seemed like hours, and the word 'cut' kept coming into my brain but not my ears. Running out of steam, invention and vocal power, I suddenly stopped. 'Do you think that's enough?', I ventured. Tony, who had been enjoying himself hugely at my obvious discomfiture (and getting exactly the sort of crap act he wanted) was not pleased. 'Why have you stopped? You don't stop acting until I say 'Cut'.' In the finished film there are about five seconds (mercifully) of my bird impression act.

Moral *As the man said, don't come out of character until the director says 'Cut'.*

On another film of Tony's *A Taste of Honey* I was asked to dub the voice of the black sailor, who fathered Jo's child. The actor who played the part, Paul Danquah, although physically right for the part, had a rather educated voice (hardly surprising for

a lawyer). Tony wanted a Liverpudlian accent, which I could more or less do. I was despatched to a studio in Hammersmith with Peter Yates, his then assistant, who directed me in the role. Very helpful he was too, I recall. I'd never dubbed a voice before and found it fascinating. The trick is to get a feeling for how the person might sound from the physical characteristics and body language. You are aided, too, by being able to listen to the original soundtrack on headphones, which gives you an idea of the actor's speech rhythms and breaths (though sometimes this can be an irritation). Technically you are helped by the fact that the film is broken down into short clips, and a vertical line comes across the screen from right to left as your cue comes up to start the dialogue. When the line hits the left hand side of the screen you start to speak. It was a fascinating morning's work and earned me £50.

Some months later I was invited to the Press Screening of the film, and lo and behold I found myself sitting behind the actor whose voice I'd dubbed. I was naturally curious to see his reaction to my voice from his body, but I hadn't anticipated just how agitated he would become as *I* began to speak *his* lines.

This was hardly surprising, as I learned later that no-one had bothered to tell him his voice had been dubbed! I sympathised with him later, keeping my mouth firmly shut.

Moral *Never let on to another actor that you've dubbed his voice unless you're absolutely sure he's been told by somebody else already.*

My fourth and final morality tale concerns my employment as dialogue coach to Richard Harris on the film *This Sporting Life*. One of my duties was to sit with Richard in make-up every morning, and take him through the day's dialogue; correcting his accent where possible. My employment in this capacity was dubious really because: a) Richard was an Irishman playing a Yorkshireman, b) I was a Lancashireman, and c) he never took any notice anyway.

Trying to concentrate on dialogue pronunciation at six-thirty am, suffering perhaps from late nights, was not easy; so for most of the time we simply sat and chatted while he was made up. He'd recently returned from playing opposite Marlon Brando in *Mutiny on the Bounty* and his horror stories of Mr. Brando's behaviour and attitude (particularly towards him) were fascinating. Nevertheless I sensed a slight sense of admiration in his voice when he talked of him, and either consciously or subconsciously he had learned a lot from him; in some ways he had even come to resemble him. This resemblance was accentuated by his insistence on having his nose, which was crooked, 'puttied' straight, and by having his hair combed forward.

One morning, thinking I was paying him a compliment, I ventured to suggest that he looked rather like Brando. His reaction to this remark was rather like that of a bull to a very large red flag waving at point blank range. To say he was displeased is an understatement. He went hoof-raging off to the director, and gave him such a hard time that I was nearly thrown off the film. If Lindsay Anderson had been a less generous and perspicacious person I'm quite sure I would have been. Happily the whole incident was a storm in a tea-cup and I subsequently became Lindsay's assistant when he directed Richard in *Diary of a Madman* at the Royal Court.

Moral *If you feel impelled to hand out a compliment to the star of the show, in the hope that it will enhance your standing in his eyes, make sure it's of a kind he will appreciate, or you could end up shooting yourself in the foot!*

Thirty years on, I was delighted that Lindsay agreed to talk to me about the film business as it relates to actors. Having read what I've written about agents he thought I'd been far too kind, and waded straight in:

Lindsay Agents make deals. Now this is perhaps not true if they get a youngster, I mean someone new to the profession, but in general at least for the first six months or even a year the agent will think of them in relation to work. If they get someone established they probably won't; they'll wait for the offers to come in. But the other thing I think it's important to remember is that agents are only aware of their clients for about six months, or perhaps a little longer but after that they tend to give up on them, they forget about them. If they are an instant hit they may take a little trouble. You can tell I don't think anything of agents. Agents are usually, I think, over flattered, and everybody writes about them, or interviews them as if they were Leland Hayward or Myron Selznick. On the whole agents are not this. On the whole agents are very lazy. I think it's probably true that for the young actor, perhaps, agents tend to be better than with anyone who's established. Because if you're established they don't try very hard.

M.T. And also the actor generates his own work once he gets known to the producers and directors.

Lindsay Well he does generate his own work, *but*, it's too often taken as an excuse by the agent who can say 'Oh he generates his own work', so he doesn't do anything. One thing I would say is that if a young actor gets an agent, if he isn't really satisfying him, he shouldn't worry about changing. Too many actors are worried, I think, about changing agents.

M.T. Because they attach too much importance to them?

Lindsay Yes. The truth is that an agent is supposed to work for you. I remember speaking to Ralph Richardson about his agent – a very reputed name in the business. And his agent wanted me to sign up with him too. So I asked Ralph if he'd actually signed a contract with him, and he said 'Good Heavens, no. It would be like signing with the man who delivers your papers.' And he was quite right. I mean, as a very well-established actor, Ralph knew that an agent is someone who works for *you* – you don't work for the agent – though the agent likes to make you feel that you do.

M.T. Do you remember all that business with Richard and the nose that I mentioned in my 'Morality Tales'?

Lindsay (Chuckles) I do. But it was very interesting you know because Richard did, on *This Sporting Life*, take a great deal of trouble with his make-up . . . had a hair piece, dyed his hair dark, and at the beginning there was a question of whether or not he should wear dark contact lenses. And this was because he thought he ought to be like David Storey, the author of the book.

M.T. Oh really? . . . But it did make him look rather like Brando didn't it?

Lindsay Well . . . the other thing was that . . . em . . . Richard did learn from Brando – particularly from Brando's make-up man, particularly in relation to his eye make-up. So as a result he did make-up well, though he rather overdid the eyes. Never mind, people didn't notice that, and it was very successful. And I think Richard looked better in *Sporting Life* than in many of his other films.

M.T. Any, I'd say. Nor do I think he's given a better performance.

Lindsay But you see he was very, very ambitious. And as a result of *Sporting Life* he fell in with American agents. And at one time Richard did say to me, when he wanted to do *Wuthering Heights* – of course he wanted to play Heathcliff, and he'd have been very good too – and David Storey did write a draft. But then he said, and I'll always remember this, he said 'Look, at this stage in my career I can't afford to make another *Sporting Life*.' And I could hear the American agent saying to him (puts on appropriate accent) 'You know Richard, at this stage in your career, I mean . . . *Sporting Life*

... great performance ... but er .. now you know you've got to do something *mainstream*.' (Pause) Who is to say he wasn't right? ... He went and made a film with Doris Day; he made a number of movies ... in the end he replaced Richard Burton in *Camelot*, on stage. And he is now, I suppose, a millionaire ... so ... I don't feel I can say he was wrong, as the liberal critic *would*... And I think if that's what he wanted, he got it. But of course, we can say, in a way it was a pity.

M.T. It's very difficult, I know, for any director to give advice to any actor coming into the business, but suppose you've got some small parts for youngsters in a film you're about to direct, tell me how you'd set about it?

Lindsay Well the importance of the casting director can't be over estimated. Most directors depend a great deal on them ... Not that the casting director casts the part, but the casting director will bring in people who she – usually a woman – has seen. I think that very often there isn't much that the actor can *do*, because the actor or actress ... well they are what they are, and I think that the impact of their personality is extremely strong. And, although I don't count myself representative, for my own part I wouldn't want to work with someone I didn't like.

M.T. Of course not, neither would I. It follows then that you must work with a casting director you like and whose judgement you respect?

Lindsay Yes, this is absolutely true. Then you can say it's important for the actors to get to know casting directors. It's a very important relationship.

M.T. They are more important than agents?

Lindsay (with no doubt whatsoever) Oh Ye-es. Much more. I have a low opinion of agents. And it's unfortunate that usually when they send round lists of clients they get put ...

M.T. In the bin?

Lindsay Yes. And generally it's because the agent thinks just in terms of age and sex, and doesn't put more into it than that. Talking on a high level, where care is taken about the casting of small parts, I think it's unfortunate that some of the new generation of directors don't really know much about actors – they don't know much about directing either – and this applies particularly to television. They want to see, or be sure of the final performance, as soon as they meet the actor, which is stupid. Therefore confidence is hugely important. If you haven't got confidence then it's just bad luck. There's nothing I can say about it, because in fact many very good actors just aren't confident. But I suppose the important thing is that if you don't get a part you mustn't feel you are responsible for this. If you don't get a job it's usually bad luck. It may well be a stupidity on the part of the director . . . It's very important that a young actor should feel that, and doesn't feel knocked in any way by not getting a part that he knows he could play terribly well.

M.T. Hopefully one becomes inured to rejection with experience.

Lindsay I remember – taking a different tack – that when we were at the Royal Court Theatre we did general auditions . . . and I remember saying to Miriam Brickman (a legendary casting director) we should have lights put up on the front of the circle, so that the actors could see them, saying 'We are suffering too'. I mean it's all a question of confidence. Actors should realize that very often the person who's interviewing them is just as nervous as they are. We're all insecure.

M.T. Exactly. Because you might make a mistake in your casting and then regret it later.

Lindsay I know . . . and I must repeat that question of confidence and belief in yourself, because so often, particularly today with the explosion of television, you will deal with directors or casting directors who are completely stupid. And I can only say that that's just bad luck, and you must not in any way let your confidence be diminished by that sort of experience.

M.T. I know that you are one of those rare animals, quote, 'an actor's director' . . .

Lindsay Possibly . . .

M.T. But you would consider yourself one, surely – as opposed to a 'technical director' . . .?

Lindsay Oh Yes . . .

M.T. . . . because you like to get performances from people. So . . . would you expect, say an actor playing a very small part in a film . . . I mean would it be alright for him to come up to you and say 'Look I'm a bit unhappy about what I'm supposed to be doing . . .' Would you feel he was getting in your hair . . . or how would you react?

Lindsay Oh no. You must accept and indeed encourage that. And that's why the English tradition of, you know, 'Do what you're told and don't bump into the furniture', is rubbish. And to make fun of people who want to know what their motivations are – they don't want to be pretentious about it . . . but if it's a genuine enquiry . . . in fact I remember, for instance, *many* years ago, I think one of the first performances that Tony Hopkins did in the West End was at the Royal Court in a production I did of *Julius Caesar*. And Tony Hopkins was playing . . . er . . . one of the conspirators; and he did come up to me in rehearsal and say, 'Why am I doing this. I don't know what the motivation of the character *is*.' Now I'd probably been remiss in not going through this, but after all Shakespeare is not very clear or detailed of what the motivations of the conspirators *are*. . .

M.T. . . . They're a mob . . .

Lindsay They're a mob, exactly. But . . . when Tony Hopkins *did* say this to me, I felt it was my duty to give him some kind of an answer that would satisfy him. Er . . . I don't in any way remember what we said, but at least it was necessary to give him a feeling that we were doing something serious, and that he wasn't just being wheeled on to say the lines. And I think that was an element in *him* which indicated that he was a good actor . . . or would *become* a good actor.

M.T. Which indeed he did.

Lindsay Which he did. He is a good actor.

M.T. I suppose, in England anyway, your best known films are *If, This Sporting Life* and *Britannia Hospital* . . .

Lindsay . . . Possibly *Oh Lucky Man*, or *The Whales of August* . . . I've no idea . . . but there aren't many.

M.T. What films have you made in America?

Lindsay I've only made *The Whales of August* . . . and I made a mini series called *Glory, Glory*, which was an American production but was made in Toronto. The leading three actors were American, Richard Thomas, James Whitmore, and Ellen Greene – the rest were all Canadian and we cast them all through meeting them and readings, or auditions – we had a casting director in Toronto.

M.T. Did you find any appreciable differences working over there than here?

Lindsay No. I think that the actors were very professional, and perhaps sometimes better prepared than the English. They took their job very seriously. They were very prepared. I wouldn't say anything more than that. I can't claim really to have made American films, because *The Whales of August* was a very small cast; it wasn't a Hollywood film. There can be a certain amateurishness on the part of the English sometimes . . .

M.T. In regard to film?

Lindsay In regard to anything actually . . . There can be.

M.T. And yet we're supposed to be the nation which produces the quality actors.

Lindsay Well, that's mostly journalism don't you think?

M.T. (slightly at a loss) . . . Yes . . . possibly . . . I mean *I* just find that there are some actors I like working with because they work hard and some I don't, irrespective of nationality. And sometimes I think 'Oh Christ what on earth was I doing when I cast *that* part.'

Lindsay Well I haven't done all that much, I mean . . . compared to Peter Hall . . . but it's not often that I've cast somebody wrongly, but there's been a couple of times when I've had to get rid of an actor . . . which is a very, very, painful experience.

Shooting the climax of *If*

M.T. Is that because they weren't shaping up, or you weren't getting on with them, or . . .?

Lindsay Yes, all those things. And it's very painful; and you must always remember it's the director's fault. You've done the casting; you've made the choice, and if it doesn't work out it's your fault. But in the end there's nothing else you can do – because what matters is the product.

M.T. Is there any point young actors writing directly to directors they *think* might be casting a film. You're probably going to say no, but tell me.

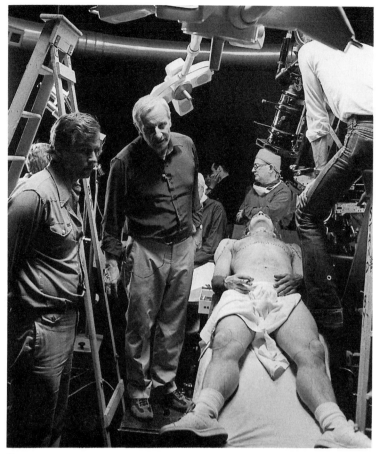

Shooting *Britannia Hospital*. Mike Fash (cameraman) on left; Lindsay Anderson (director) in centre; Mike Roberts (camera operator – on overhead camera); Malcolm McDowell on bed

Lindsay There's very little point, but I don't think it ever does any harm . . . Agents will usually say 'Oh, don't do that, leave it to me' . . . but if a young actor writes to me and sends a photograph . . .

M.T. Do you reply?

Lindsay Well I . . .

M.T. No, don't answer that or you'll be deluged!

Lindsay Well you're right. It isn't likely to result in anything. But I think that that, shall we say, 'Get up and Go' spirit is important. And I think that it's important that the young actor or actress knows that it *is* up to them. Don't expect too much, but don't resign too much responsibility entirely to your agent, thinking they'll look after it. Because probably the truth is they probably won't. But you have to do these things intelligently. You have to know who you're writing to, and what you're writing *about* . . . Don't completely rely on that publication that says something's being made or prepared . . . what's it called?

M.T. P.C.R. (Professional Casting Report, a U.K. publication)

Lindsay That's right. I mean it's all very useful, but their information is only as good as its informants; and they're often wrong.

M.T. Have you got any final thoughts for young actors?

Lindsay I think it's important to be yourself. Realise you will run up against difficulties, particularly today in television, you may have to do everything for yourself. Many young directors who come in from university, know absolutely nothing about dealing with actors. Of course if this was a book addressed to directors there are many things that one could say. One of the things would be that half of them shouldn't be doing it anyway! Ah well . . . just tell them that it's a very difficult business.

Chapter Ten
Concerning Comedy

'Sitcom is a sod!', the words of my tutor at the BBC, when I was on the television director's course twenty-five years ago still ring in my ears. 'The trouble is it's neither fish nor fowl, theatre or television'.

Years later I came to appreciate what he meant as I tackled my first sitcom series. But adrenalin kept me going and doubtless it will have the same effect on you, and bring you back for more, it's addictive.

Actors have to perform for both the studio audience, who have often travelled miles to be entertained, and the unseen audience at home. And, as we've discussed earlier, playing in the theatre is so very different from playing on the screen. The actor is faced with a dilemma – if he goes for a full-bloodied performance he may be much appreciated by the studio audience, and raise the laughs they are there to provide; too muted a performance won't raise a titter, but may be acclaimed by the television critics (who may be surprised by the lack of audience response). At the end of the day it's back to instinct and a mutual trust between yourself and the director. If he says 'A bit OTT' (over the top), and you think his judgement sound, take it down a bit. The bottom line is that you must gauge your performance to your audiences (both of them!).

David Jason, who I first met and worked with nearly thirty years ago, has emerged, after years of hard slog, as one of the leading comedy actors of the day; he was given public recognition for his enormous contribution to our enjoyment by being awarded the OBE in 1993. His experience of acting in all branches of the profession is unique and varied, and I am extremely grateful to him for agreeing to answer a few questions and share his thoughts with us. I asked him what he thought was the basic difference between playing in a sitcom with an audience, and playing a comedy role on film, without one.

Jason A studio audience is extremely intrusive; acting to it is very difficult because you also have to serve the audience which will be in front of you – I mean on screen – you can't stand around for 20 minutes trying to absorb a laugh, as you can on stage – you have to get on with it. On the other hand doing comedy *without* an audience is extremely difficult. It requires a great deal of experience to pull it off and get the best laughs – you have to have your comedy timing locked in the back of your brain . . . it comes with experience.

M.T. So have you got to imagine an audience laughing at home when they see it, almost pre-judge when they're going to laugh and then leave an appropriate amount of time?

Jason You're right. In the back of your mind you do have to be aware of how the show will be cut together. For instance, when you say a funny line you've got to leave enough space, for either your own, or somebody else's reaction, before you continue. Whereas when you have a live audience, they will tell you – they'll laugh and then you wait, as you do in the theatre.

M.T. But if you're doing, say, *Darling Buds of May* on film, it's all very well for you, as an actor, to leave what you think is the right length of pause for a laugh, but you've got no control over the editing. If you get an awful director who can cut your pause out because he doesn't think it's right, there's nothing you can do about that is there? Because you don't have any editorial control do you?

Jason (After a wry pause) Well . . . what you hope is that most of the directors that you work with are experienced and good enough to let it go out the way you've done it.

M.T. And if they're not?

Jason I'm afraid there is nothing you can do about that. You have to leave the pause that you think is right, then leave it to them. And sometimes you think 'bloody hell, he's cut that out'. But you have to bite the bullet and not get yourself worked up and get on the 'phone and make a scene. You have to say 'I win some, I lose some'. Otherwise you find yourself getting into a battle with the director for editorial control and make yourself, eventually, extremely unwelcome.

M.T. You'd get a bad reputation for interfering?

Jason Yes, you would. That's not the way to work, it's not creative. If you're allowed your opinion you say, 'I'm sorry, I really didn't think that worked because you cut such and such away', which I have done many a time. And if I see something before it goes out, which I don't think works, I'm usually listened to.

M.T. But only because you're a 'star' now.

Jason I suppose so . . . Mind you I only make comments after I've seen the 'off-line' (preparatory edit) . . . But I always criticise *myself* first . . . I always have . . . I think you should make that point Malcolm. It's no use actors slagging off the director, or anyone else for that matter, without first taking a very close look at what they themselves have been up to.

M.T. I take your point . . . Suppose when you're doing a show, you realise, perhaps by 'clocking' a monitor, that something could work better visually, would you make your thoughts known?

Jason Sure. I'll ask to have a word with the director and explain that I think, for example, a reaction shot, say, put in here would help the comic moment, and because I very rarely make any comments, they tend to listen . . . I might have a bit more clout now, but it wasn't always the case; remember I started in rep . . . One of the things I think is that you have to be philosophical and retain your concentration and drive . . . (after some thought) You see the director has to help the audience see where the joke is . . . to centre it. We're all part of the same creative team. All working *together*.

M.T. Good point . . . now talking about 'togetherness' – comedy needs more 'two shots' than most dramas, right?

Jason Yes, it's nice to watch interaction. Comedy, unless it's stand up comedy, is always reactive; 'character' comedy;

Richard Wilson and Annette Crosbie in a classic 'two shot' from *One Foot in the Grave,* surrounded by small friends

always about people, or environment, not about one bloke being funny and everyone else being straight. You need the other people to correspond to, to counter-react . . . when he says something funny, we want to see the other bloke too. In *One Foot in the Grave* – when the two leads are together they exploit the two shot beautifully . . .'

M.T. I always remember, I learnt a lot about this from watching *Morecombe and Wise*; the two-shots . . . that's what I remember visually . . . So by and large, do you prefer playing comedy to an audience or without one?

Jason I used to very much enjoy playing to an audience. It's much more satisfying to get a big laugh, but it's very stressful too. You worry about why certain things did or didn't get a laugh. You're constantly worrying and working things out. Then there's the rush of adrenalin when there's a live audience in the studio. You get a heightened performance; it's not the same performance you'd give on film because it has much more energy.

M.T. So you now prefer working on film, without an audience? Even though your performance level might be marginally down? Or do you try to counteract that?

Jason Yes I do. But it's difficult because film is . . . well, trying to be much more realistic, so your performance level has to go down a bit . . . so that you are *in* reality, and not playing a heightened reality. Comedy is played at a different level without an audience unless it's a madcap farce . . . whereas sitcom is *plainly* not real because the audience are in a studio laughing . . . so there's a slight edge of *un*reality which I think you need to make it work . . . God, it's complicated this in'it? (wipes brow and chuckles)

M.T. If there were a young actor playing a small part in *Only Fools and Horses*, what advice would you give him or her?

Jason Look, learn, mark, and inwardly digest! All I could really advise is – always be at every rehearsal. Ask to come in, even if it's not your scene. You can see the way people work, their attitude. And if you've got a good company, it educates you as to how to behave, how to interact, perhaps, with a director. I don't know how other people work – I certainly wouldn't want people stamping around, throwing scripts, rowing and shouting. In my experience, that's never happened, and if it did I would walk away from it. If you feel that the stars of the show you're in are worth watching, then seize the moment because the opportunity doesn't present itself very often. You may not get another part for six months. So the learning process is so bloody short – one week's rehearsal!

M.T. Apart from watching, how should a young actor behave in relation to the stars of the show?

Jason I think with extremely good manners – some of our more established actors don't suffer fools gladly; you certainly don't slap them on the back and say 'Alright pal?' Politeness, care and consideration . . . 'How do you think David Jason likes to be referred to?' for example, and you'd find out that they all call me David. (Chuckles) One star of yesteryear always used to insist on being addressed as 'Mr. Charles' . . . So, if you've got any intelligence, you find out how to approach the star.

M.T. How important is the script in a comedy? Would you take a script just because it was a super part or would you look beyond that?

Jason No, not any more. I used to do anything at one time because I wanted to work and develop my skills. Now I have to look at the whole thing. But there's no guarantee a show will be a success. If we all knew the answers we'd all be millionaires. Personally I really look at the script first, and then, of course the part. You're right that if I don't like the script then I won't take the part. But as I said before, if you're starting out you should take everything you're offered.

M.T. So that's your advice to young actors – take more or less anything that comes up for the experience?

Jason Yes of course; because I believe you're learning about yourself. You're communicating with people. Also you meet other actors . . . directors, writers and . . . you know someone might say 'listen I've got this project . . .' So you can meet, talk about things . . . instead of sitting in your ivory tower waiting for a casting director to give you a job – they have to have seen your work . . . if you sit about for too long there won't be any of your work to see!

M.T. When you're creating a new character, has there ever been a time, when it comes to playing that part, when, if you're honest with yourself, you don't really have it under your belt?

Jason I don't think a character is ever fully fledged for me in the first few days of filming, because we have virtually no rehearsals. I think rehearsals are bloody essential. They shouldn't be considered a luxury, but a necessity. I'm afraid people are trying to take away actors' rehearsal periods all the time, because they're not actors and they don't understand their problems. This is mainly because of budgets. Accountants are running things, and trying to save money.

With *Darling Buds of May* we had a week's rehearsal before each episode, where we moved it around and actually discussed scenes; which was great and was one of the reasons why it worked.

M.T. What about *A Touch of Frost?*

Jason The powers that be didn't want to have any rehearsals and we had to protest. They quoted other shows, such as *Morse*, which I believe didn't rehearse. Our suggestions weren't resisted but it had to come from me, they wouldn't have accepted it from anyone else. I said I was insecure about playing it without rehearsals. If two actors disagree about the way to play a scene, how can you expect to get the scene right? You need to have mutual agreement with the director about the shape of a scene . . . where the moments are . . . what should be centred, what should be underlined, what information you want to give away, etc. On *Frost*, for instance, we try not to give too much away – we try to *tease* the audience . . . If a show starts getting too heavy I remind people that we're not making a documentary, we're making a piece of entertainment. So we bear that in mind.

M.T. Having gone through the rehearsal period, have you ever still not been happy when you were turning over actual footage?

Jason That happens on most things on film. The first few days are 'finding', but I learn very quickly. But really it's a pretty hairy thing . . . but I got more confident with *Frost* as the show progressed. I understood what he could and couldn't do. As I relaxed, I could afford to take a bit more risk with the lighter moments. Not back off and always aim for the drama. A lot of midnight oil was burned in close discussion with the director.

M.T. Yes, I felt that in the first episode that you were so determined not to give any suggestion that it was David Jason 'comedy actor', that perhaps you didn't relax quite as much as you did in the second or third episode.

Jason Quite right. But you also do that in the theatre don't you? And nobody questions that. It's no different really. Over

David Jason, as Inspector Frost, frowns in concentration between takes

the course of a run, a character grows and develops. Certainly for the first two months, as you work with an audience, you realise where the laughs come in. So it's a learning process that never stops – unfortunately in television you don't get enough time. Young people coming in can't learn it all from drama school . . . (wry smile) mind you, some of them think they can!

M.T. You never went to drama school. When you first came into the business, did you ever feel any way inferior to people who did?

Jason Totally. I always thought everyone was better than me.

M.T. Drama school does give you more confidence. I think it's a good idea to go if it's possible.

Jason That's exactly what the people are doing today. I wouldn't advise anybody to come into the business who's not been to drama school – because they turn out these nearly professional people, full of confidence, which is quite good for them. But today you have no way of getting yourself into the business – easing in – you now have to go to casting directors who ask you 'Where have you been and what have you been doing?' – if you say 'Joe Soap's Amateur Spud Bashing Factory', they send you back on the tube – you see their argument would be that people who have been to drama school deserve to be taken more seriously than those who haven't because they've definitely decided to make acting their career, and aren't just playing at it. So you really have no chance now. You can't do a little job in rep anymore and sweep the stage and eventually get to play the lead – those jobs just don't exist . . . So in my opinion, these days you have to go to drama school.

M.T. Don't you make any exception at all for people, say, who have been to Oxford and Cambridge?

Jason Ah . . . yes . . well, my answer to that has to be 'yes'. But we are talking about an elitist group. They tend to use their cerebral powers by playing with words – and they also tend to do comedy of a different sort to mine.

M.T. So basically what you're saying is either drama school or a university with a strong drama reputation?

Jason Yes. Those are the two professional systems. You have to show some sort of intelligence and effort to get into university, and you have to show some sort of talent and ability to get into RADA or wherever.

M.T. Yet you didn't go to either, and you've 'made it'. You don't think you would have if you were coming in now?

Jason (Long pause) It would be much more difficult . . . I think, to be honest. At the end of the day . . . if it *burns* in you . . . if it's worth more that life itself, then do it! Because you've *got* to do it. And you'll fight tooth and nail. That's different. Dedication has got to be monk-like if you really want to be an actor. You can't just say 'I think I'll be an actor, and one day I'll be a star because me mum thinks I'm brilliant' . . . All I'm saying that it's *nearly* impossible without proper training.

M.T. But, tell me honestly – do you think the spur of feeling inferior at not going through the conventional channels has helped you to be as successful as you are?

Jason . . . I suppose so. I love the business more than anything else. But I dedicated myself to every job I did, I wanted to try to improve, be better. That meant entertaining the people more, getting more laughs, inventing bits of business, making sure that the audience out there got it. I had a piece of advice once, which held me in tremendously good stead. I was playing Gentleman Starkey in *Peter Pan* and Ron Moody was playing Hook. I had to do a front cloth scene while they changed the set behind; it was traditional. We'd been playing for three weeks and I couldn't get a laugh to save my life. We were out there every night for 4–6 minutes, no laughs. Every time I tried to do something different, the director would come round and go bananas and tell me to do it as written. One night I came out and it was so bad . . . full house, and not even a titter . . . So I went to see Ron and asked him to give me some jokes. 'Do you want to do it as the director told you or as the audience tells you?', he asked, 'If you're so worried about getting laughs, you have to do it yourself, because *my* jokes won't be *yours*.' I was very disappointed because I thought he would save my life, not give me a lecture. But by the time I got from his dressing room to mine, I understood what he was saying. I was determined from that moment on that I would make that front cloth work.

Three months later, when we were finishing the tour, I came off on the last night to hoots of laughter, rounds of applause. I walked past the director, who was in the wings, gobsmacked, and he patted me on the shoulders and said 'Dave, that was absolutely brilliant, I've never seen anything so wonderful, you've done miracles there'. He said that to my back, because I never stopped walking. If I'd have stopped, I might have told him what I thought of him. He'd given me no help or encouragement – he'd virtually destroyed me. Ron Moody saved me.

Ron taught me the biggest lesson of my life. The most important people, certainly in comedy, are the audience. It's more difficult to debate that in drama because you rely on the skills of the director to interpret how much the audience is receiving. But comedy is different . . . it doesn't mean that you ride rough-shot over everybody and do your own thing, certainly not in television. But as a piece of advice, it's the audience that you must listen to, because they tell you if you've got it . . . Mind you some anarchy works – Rik Mayall in *Bottom* – but Rick Mayall and his partner have created a new genre. But young actors starting out . . . shouldn't try to be as anarchic as him . . . (chuckles) . . . because he's a one off!

M.T. If there was just one piece of advice that you could give to somebody who wanted to come into the business, particularly to play comedy, what would be your parting shot?

Jason It ain't gonna be easy; nothing worthwhile ever is . . . and you must *enjoy it*. If you haven't got the ability to laugh and enjoy your career, you might as well go and be a . . . a politician!

Most sitcoms are usually recorded in bursts of 6, 7 or the full 13 episodes which comprise a 'series', for the Spring, Autumn or Winter schedules (Summer traditionally being reserved for re-runs of the 'tried and trusted').

Filmed (or increasingly taped these days) exterior inserts are usually done before the main studio shoot begins, and this is where you can come unstuck. Very often there will be no prior rehearsal period to this filming, so you had better make sure you know exactly what sort of characterisation you're going to give before you arrive on location, or you might lumber yourself when you try to continue the performance in the studio, perhaps weeks later. There's no going back if you decide he shouldn't have a limp after all. Make sure, if rehearsals are denied, that you at least get the opportunity to have a good natter with the director about your part. This is an essential pre-requisite, and often forgotten.

The recording schedule is arduous – usually an episode a week, and may go something like this: Sunday off – Monday rehearse – Tuesday rehearse – Wednesday rehearse – Thursday run through followed by producer's technical run. Friday camera rehearsals all morning, two straight runs on camera in the afternoon (one as in the theatre, a 'dress' run), a short supper break, then record with an audience from 7.30 – 10 pm. Saturday morning block next week's episode. The actors then have Sunday at home to learn their lines – in theory!

Rehearsal hours are often shorter than those for conventional drama because it's harder to concentrate on comedy for longer than a few hours (personally I like to rehearse from 10.30 – 2pm, with no lunch break). There's another thing to be taken into consideration, the timing of rehearsals, so that actors reach their peak on the recording day; too little and they're ill-prepared, too much and they're past their sell-by date. The shorter hours also give the director an opportunity to construct the all important camera script during reasonable working hours. Unlike soaps and such, it's impossible to pre-plan a shot list before you have done at least a couple of rehearsals because so much creativity comes from the actors' invention. I also like to incorporate a speed 'word run', on, say, the Wednesday and Thursday mornings, before rehearsals; it makes the actors aware which lines, if any, they've remembered of the ones they'd forgotten yesterday!

If you're used to acting in the theatre you should feel quite at home on the studio day; what with costume and make-up calls, 'dress runs' and 'director's notes', you will feel you are being geared up to do a one-night stand, which of course, you are.

The theatrical atmosphere, immediately prior to recording, will be heightened even more once the audience have taken their seats and the 'warm-up' man takes over. They are often stand up comics (though some producers and some stars like to do their own). Although these people are supposed to foster a sense of fun and jollity among the audience, it doesn't always work out that way. I remember having to get rid of a chap after he stunned the audience into abject silence with the following bad taste one-liner; 'How do you tell an incontinent alcoholic? – Rusty zip' . . . Exactly, that was their reaction too!

You might like doing audience shows because there are so

few technicalities to get in the way of your communication with the director. There are usually few, if any, special effects, other than mechanical ones, to worry about, and the shooting is comparatively simple. Retakes can be a drag, as it's hard to persuade an audience to laugh at the same joke twice – but all in all, if you like playing comedy, you might find yourself having a ball. At least it's the one area in television where the actor retains control of his talent; unlike scowling to order in a thriller, or beaming inanely in a commercial.

Chapter Eleven
Fast Fade

Well that seems to be about it. But I have a final thought. After my chat with Lindsay Anderson we went off to a neighbourhood Trattoria for lunch. I hadn't been in his company on a one to one basis for many years and our relationship was as warm and amicable as I remembered it used to be – just as if we had met regularly over the years and had become close friends. 'Lindsay', I said 'I can't tell you how reassuring it is to meet up with someone I haven't met for ages, who has achieved outstanding success and plaudits, and who hasn't changed one jot from the early days of ambition and struggle.'

Of course I meant by that that his genuine *personal* demeanour and friendliness hadn't changed, not his professional attitude to the business, which, of course, has been coloured in the light of his own experience.

I then went on to tell him a few horror stories of others I had encountered whose success seemed to have turned them into unapproachable egocentric monsters. (And if you haven't yet experienced the awful fright of such an encounter, you surely will!) He looked hard and long at me, smiled benignly, and said, 'But my dear Malcolm, don't you realise that the successful people you've just mentioned haven't suddenly changed into monsters – they always were. It's just that they hid their true natures from view until they considered they were in a position to reveal them.'

There's a little prayer I often say (and I'm not an overtly religious person) which is worth setting down because it might help you if you feel the stresses of the business are getting you down: *God grant me the serenity to accept the things I cannot change, courage to change the things I can, and the wisdom to know the difference.*

Think about it. And great good luck.

Appendix 1
Useful Addresses

Equity

British Actors Equity
Association; (head office)
Guild House
Upper St. Martin's Lane
London WC2H 9EG
Tel. 071 379 6000
Fax. 071 379 7001

N.B. to safeguard the professional standing of artists, duplication of names is not allowed. Please check with the Equity Office.

The Equity staff will be happy to deal with any queries about the status of any Theatre Company or other employer or answer any queries about membership or other contractual matters.

British Equity
(Wales, South West England and West Midlands)
Transport House
1 Cathedral Road
Cardiff CF1 9SD

British Equity
(Northern England)
12 Blackfriars St
Salford
Manchester M3 5BQ

British Equity
(Scotland and Northern Ireland)
65 Bath Street
Glasgow G3 2BX

Screen Actors Guild (SAG)
National Headquarters,
3601 West Olive Avenue,
P.O. Box 7830
Burbank
California
USA

Contacts and The Spotlight

The names and addresses of theatrical managements, theatre, opera and ballet companies and other useful information can be found in *Contacts*. *The Spotlight* is the pictorial casting guide for actors. Both publications are available from 7 Leicester Place, London WC2H 7BP.

Dance and Drama School Courses

For information about dance and drama school training, and a list of currently accredited courses, please write to (with SAE):

The Secretary
Council for Dance Education
and Training
Riverside Studios
Crisp Road
London W6 9RL

The Secretary
National Council for Drama
Training
5 Tavistock Place
London WC1 9SS

N.C.D.T. Accredited Courses

Academy of Live and Recorded
Arts
The Royal Victoria Building,
Trinity Road,
London SW18 3SX

Arts Educational Schools
Drama Department,
14 Bath Road,
London W4 1LY

Birmingham School of Speech
Training and Drama
45 Church Road,
Edgbaston,
Birmingham B15 3SW

Bristol Old Vic Theatre School
1/2 Downside Road,
Clifton,
Bristol BS8 2XF

Central School of Speech and
Drama
Embassy Theatre,
64 Eton Ave,
Swiss Cottage,
London NW3 3HY

Drama Centre London
176 Prince of Wales Road,
London NW5 3PT

Drama Studio
Grange Court,
1 Grange Road,
London W5 5QN

Guildford School of Acting and
Dance
Millmead Terrace,
Guildford,
Surrey GU2 5AT

Guildhall School of Music and
Dramatic Art
Silk Street,
Barbican,
London EC2Y 8DT

LAMDA
Tower House,
226 Cromwell Road,
London SW5 0SR

Manchester Polytechnic School
of Theatre
The Capitol Building,
School Lane,
Didsbury,
Manchester M20 0HT

Mountview Theatre School
104 Crouch Hill,
London N8 9EA

Rose Burford College of Speech
& Drama
Lamorbey Park,
Sidcup,
Kent DA15 9DF

Royal Academy of
Dramatic Art
62–64 Gower Street,
London WC1E 6ED

Royal Scottish Academy of
Music and Drama
100 Renfrew Street,
Glasgow G2 3DB

Webber Douglas Academy of
Dramatic Art
30–36 Clareville Street,
London SW7 5AP

Welsh College of Music and
Drama
Castle Grounds,
Cathays Park,
Cardiff, CF1 3ER

N.B. Accreditation applies to specific courses only, not the drama school as a whole. Please contact the drama school for further information.

Write direct to the school for a copy of their prospectus. Most prefer applicants to be at least 18 years old. 'A' levels are not normally essential.

Grant Aid Information

A student's most likely source of grant aid to study at drama school is the Local Education Authority. If there is a Drama Adviser for the area, it is as well to seek their advice.

Grants for drama training are discretionary, not mandatory.

The following publications give information on other possible sources of grant aid. Copies can be found at local reference libraries.

Student Grants and Loans – A brief guide and *Postgraduate Awards – state bursaries for graduate study on designated professional and vocational courses*
Available from Awards and Loans Group, Further and Higher Education Branch 3, Department of Education, Mowden Hall, Staindrop Road, Darlington, Co. Durham DL3 9BG

The Charities Digest
Available from The Family Welfare Association, 501–505 Kingsland Road, London E8 4AU

Directory of Grant Making Trusts
Available from the Charities Aid Foundation, 48 Pembury Road, Tunbridge, Kent TN9 2JD

The Grants Register
Available from Macmillan Distribution Ltd, Brunel Road, Houndmills, Basingstoke RG21 2XS

Appendix 2
Equity Entry Requirements

Guide to Entry

Membership of Equity is open to anyone currently exercising professional skills in the provision of entertainment.

To be eligible to apply, you must supply proof of a current contract, as approved by Equity and details of any professional engagements. An application form for Provisional membership will then be sent to you to complete. This should be returned, with the entrance fee and annual subscription. Your application will then be placed before the Equity Council.

In certain areas of work, only artists with previous professional experience or those who can be included within an agreement quota of newcomers to the profession can normally be considered for work.

Newcomers to the profession do not usually enter through television, commercials, film or radio, where evidence of previous professional experience is required. Newcomers also do not enter as performers or stage management through the West End Theatre or the Royal National Theatre or as Stage Managers or Deputy Stage Managers in other areas of theatre. These engagements are normally only given to performers or stage management with at least 30 weeks professional experience. (Full membership of Equity is accepted as proof of such experience and this status is obtained after serving as a Provisional member for 30 weeks and having acquired the equivalent amount of professional experience).

N.B. Work as a Background, Supporting or Walk-On Artist in television or commercials or as a Crowd Artist or Stand-In in films is not accepted as professional experience.

Membership of Equity may be obtained through engagements in the following areas of work:

Theatre

As a performer or Assistant Stage Manager in: a Subsidised Repertory Company, a Theatre-In-Education or Young People's Theatre Company, a Provincial Commercial Sessional Work Company (usually

Children's Theatre) or a Non-Subsidised Repertory Company under the quotas of newcomer places agreed with the Theatrical Management Association.

As a performer in a Provincial Commercial Summer Season, Pantomime or Tour under the quota of newcomers.

As an ASM, with no obligation to act or understudy, in a Provincial Commercial Summer Season, Pantomime or Tour.

As a performer or ASM in a Small-Scale Theatre Company which has a quota of newcomer places agreed with the Independent Theatre Council.

As a performer with the Royal Shakespeare Company at Stratford-upon-Avon or with the Chichester Festival Theatre under the agreed newcomer quotas.

Opera and Ballet

As a Singer engaged by an Opera Company as a Chorister, Principal Singer or Guest Artist engaged on the appropriate contract.

As a Dancer with a Ballet or Dance Company on the Ballet contract.

As an Assistant Stage Manager with an Opera or Ballet company on the Stage Management contract.

Directors, Designers or Choreographers

As a Director, Designer or Choreographer engaged on the appropriate contract for work in the theatre.

Variety or Circus

As a Variety Artist, in which case you will need to be able to prove that you have been engaged on at least **eight** separate occasions, for which you have been paid an appropriate professional fee. The application will first be considered by the Variety Branch nearest your permanent address, which will make a recommendation to the Equity Council on your application.

As a Circus Artist engaged on an appropriate contract.

As a Dancer engaged in a Cabaret Floorshow on an appropriate contract or with an Overseas dance troupe engaged on the appropriate Overseas Contract.

Other Categories

As a Professional Broadcaster in television or radio.

As a Concert or Session Singer when you will need to be able to prove that you have been engaged on a number of separate occasions on a professional basis at an appropriate professional fee in these categories of work.

Work Overseas

If you have worked professionally overseas and can provide proof of your employment, together with details of membership, if any, of the relevant union in the countries concerned, you may be granted exemption from the Casting Agreements. This will mean that, depending on the length of your professional experience abroad, you will be entitled to seek work in the United Kingdom as if you were an existing Equity member with comparable professional experience. This arrangement, which applies only to UK or European Community citizens or to those from other countries who have been granted permission to work in the UK as artists, will not entitle you to membership but you may apply on obtaining your first engagement in this country.

Guide to Entry for Registered Graduates

Registered Graduates are students who have successfully completed Acting or Stage Management or Dancing courses accredited by the National Council for Drama Training or the Council for Dance Education and Training.

Graduates are placed on a Register which is maintained at the Equity Office and receive a Registered Graduate card from us to show to prospective employers. Students can remain on the Register for up to two years after completing the accredited course. They are then subject to the same terms of entry that apply to non-Registered Graduates, details of which are available in a separate leaflet from Equity Offices.

N.B. Registered Graduate status is not equivalent to Equity membership, which can only be obtained after following the process described below.

(The guidelines are much the same as those for non-graduates but your attention is drawn to the asterisked clauses which do differ.)

Entry

Membership of Equity is open to anyone currently exercising professional skills in the provision of entertainment.

To be eligible to apply, you must supply proof of a current contract, as approved by Equity and details of any professional engagements. An application form for Provisional membership will then be sent to you to complete. This should be returned, with the entrance fee and annual subscription. Your application will then be placed before the Equity Council.

In certain areas of work, only artists with previous professional experience or those who can be included within an agreement quota of newcomers to the profession can normally be considered for work.

*Newcomers to the profession do not usually enter as performers or stage management through the West End Theatre or the Royal National Theatre or as Stage Managers or Deputy Stage Managers in other areas of theatre. These engagements are normally only given to performers or stage management with at least 30 weeks professional experience. (Full membership of Equity is accepted as proof of such experience and this status is obtained after serving as a Provisional member for 30 weeks and having acquired the equivalent amount of professional experience).

Entry and consequent membership of Equity may be obtained through engagements in the following areas of work:

Theatre

*As a performer or Assistant Stage Manager in: a Subsidised Repertory Company, a Theatre-In-Education or Young People's Theatre Company, a Provincial Commercial Sessional Work Company (usually Children's Theatre) or a Non-Subsidised Repertory Company. (Managers can engage any number of Registered Graduates without being subject to the newcomer quota that applies to non-registered graduates).

*As a performer in a Provincial Commercial Summer Season, Pantomime or Tour under the quota of newcomer places reserved for Registered Graduates, as agreed with the Theatrical Management Association. As a performer in a West End production, the SWET Managers having a quota of one Registered Graduate per production per annum.

As a performer or ASM in a Small-Scale Theatre Company which has a quota of newcomer places agreed with the Independent Theatre Council.

As a performer with the Royal Shakespeare Company at Stratford-upon-Avon or with the Chichester Festival Theatre under the agreed newcomer quotas.

Opera and Ballet

As a Singer engaged by an Opera Company as a Chorister, Principal Singer or Guest Artist engaged on the appropriate contract.

As a Dancer with a Ballet or Dance Company on the Ballet contract.

As an Actor with an Opera or Ballet or Dance Company on the appropriate contract.

As an Assistant Stage manager with an Opera or Ballet company on the Stage Management contract.

Directors, Designers or Choreographers

As a Director, Designer or Choreographer engaged on the appropriate contract for work in the theatre.

*Television, Films, Radio and Commercials

As a performer (other than a stunt performer) engaged on the appropriate contract.

Variety or Circus

As a Variety Artist, in which case you will need to be able to prove that you have been engaged on at least **eight** separate occasions, for which you have been paid an appropriate professional fee. The application will first be considered by the Variety Branch nearest your permanent address, which will make a recommendation to the Equity Council on your application.

As a Circus Artist engaged on an appropriate contract.

As a Dancer engaged in a Cabaret Floorshow on an appropriate contract or with an Overseas dance troupe engaged on the appropriate Overseas Contract.

Other Categories

As a Professional Broadcaster in television or radio.

As a Concert or Session Singer when you will need to be able to prove that you have been engaged on a number of separate occasions on a professional basis at an appropriate professional fee in these categories of work.

Work Overseas

If you have worked professionally overseas and can provide proof of your employment, together with details of membership, if any, of the relevant union in the countries concerned, you may be granted exemption from the Casting Agreements. This will mean that, depending on the length of your professional experience abroad, you will be entitled to seek work in the United Kingdom as if you were an existing Equity member with comparable professional experience. This arrangement, which applies only to UK or European Community citizens or to those from other countries who have been granted permission to work in the UK as artists, will not entitle you to membership but you may apply on obtaining your first engagement in this country.

N.B. To safeguard the professional standing of artists, duplication of names is not allowed. Please check with the Equity Office.

The Equity staff will be happy to deal with any queries about the status of any Theatre Company or other employer or answer any questions about membership or other contractual matters.

The current joining fee of Equity is £35, and the first year's subscription is £26. Thereafter subscriptions are calculated on earnings during the preceding year as follows:

Up to £3,000 ....£26
Between 3 & £4,000 ....£40
Between 4 & £5,000 ....£50
Between 5 & £6,000 ....£60
Between 6 & £7,000 ....£70
Between 7 & £8,000 ....£80
Between 8 & £9,000 ....£90
Between 9 & £10,000 ....£100

Subscriptions on earnings over £10,000 are calculated at 1% of earnings up to a maximum of £1,200.

Index

Guildford College
Learning Resource Centre

Please return on or before the last date shown
This item may be renewed by telephone unless overdue

1 1 MAY 2004 2 4 MAY 2011		

Class: _791.43028 TAY_

Title: _THE ACTOR AND THE CAMERA_

Author: _TAYLOR, MALCOLM_